TWO WEEKS
to
WINNING
CHESS

TWO WEEKS
to
WINNING CHESS

Adapted from the works of
FRED REINFELD
by BEATRICE REINFELD

DOUBLEDAY & COMPANY, INC.
GARDEN CITY, NEW YORK

OTHER BOOKS BY FRED REINFELD

Complete Chess Course
Chess in a Nutshell
How to Be a Winner at Chess
How to Play Better Chess

Library of Congress Catalog Card Number 75-160890
Published by special agreement with
Sterling Publishing Co., Inc.
Copyright © 1971 by Sterling Publishing Co., Inc.
© 1956 by Sterling Publishing Co., Inc.
"How to Beat Your Opponent Quickly"
© 1957 by Sterling Publishing Co., Inc.
"Reinfeld Explains Chess"
© 1961 by Fred Reinfeld
"Chess Is an Easy Game"
© 1964 by Sterling Publishing Co., Inc.
"Strategy in the Chess Endgame"

CONTENTS

INTRODUCTION

From a reader:

"I've browsed through several chess books by other authors, but invariably I have come back to Mr. Reinfeld's. I have a great appreciation for brevity and wit . . . Mr. Reinfeld has the unique ability of putting a principle down succinctly and thoroughly, with a dash of color and a slice of wit . . ."

When Fred Reinfeld taught chess at New York University he marveled at how eager his students were to play the game, and how little interested they were in studying. Week after week he would lecture on how to play the openings, the importance of development, how to take advantage of the opponent's weakness, how to recognize losing moves, everything that takes the player out of the class of total duffer into the class of winning chess player.

Although the students listened intently, what they really wanted to do was *play*, which they did—making the same kinds of mistakes they had been warned against, and missing the same advantageous moves they had been taught to recognize. And these were not ordinary run-of-the-mill students—they were doctors, lawyers, teachers, men and women high in their professions, devoted to the game of chess, frustrated by their inability to beat their opponents, and wanting to learn to improve their chess prowess!

An able teacher, Fred Reinfeld accepted the sad fact that the would-be chess player had to be taught the elements of the game in the simplest way possible. The lessons had to be uncluttered by details and yet thorough enough to help him beat players of his own class. Out of his experience with students who were not yet ready to absorb a great many details and fine points, he changed his approach in writing and turned out many volumes on all phases of the games. From these, I have adapted this book. These fourteen lessons, if studied as indicated, will not only teach you how to play the game, but how to understand what you and your opponent are doing, and why; and lastly, how to play the endgame without too much frustrating floundering.

In the first five lessons you will learn how to play a game. However, you may be baffled as to how to continue the game once you are past the opening moves and the position becomes complicated, with many options open to you. Lessons 6 to 9 go more deeply into what a chess game is. Each lesson deals with one game, analyzing it move by move, and you must study these with particular attention. In these lessons you will learn how to apply psychology to the game, how to exploit your opponent's weaknesses, when to be aggressive, when cautious, when to punish your opponent for his timidity. By studying these lessons you will gain a deeper insight into the conduct of a game than any amount of haphazard playing will give you.

Lessons 10 to 14, dealing with the endgame, are the most difficult of all and require your careful concentration. They show you how to finish a game. They answer the questions, among others, of how to win or draw when there are only Pawns and Kings left on the board; how to play endings with the various pieces; how to finish a game when neither side has a material advantage, or if you're ahead in material, or behind. What kind of ending cannot be won? How can you tell if a game which appears to be lost, can be drawn? And to wind it all up, there's a brief quiz to give you a chance to study positions from actual play, size them up, and decide what you would do to win the game. You'll be able to measure what you've learned by checking your solutions with those at the back of the book.

Fred Reinfeld always encouraged his pupils to write down their games and study them later to see what they could learn from their mistakes. I remember, with some embarrassment, I admit, once when I (a duffer) was playing with another duffer. After looking on for a few moves, Fred began to record the game, chortling and rubbing his hands gleefully as we struggled. When it was over, he played back the game for us pointing out our mistakes, counter-mistakes, missed mates, etc. He said it was the best (!) example he could ever hope to find of how *not* to play chess and was going to present it to his class the following week as an object lesson. That game is immortalized somewhere in one of his books and I am sure someone is learning from our mistakes.

Hints: It's especially important for you to study Diagram 62 showing the names of the squares, and the chess notation, because unless you have an intimate knowledge of and fluency with them, you won't be able to study these lessons easily.

Another hint: When you study games, use two chessboards, or a pocket set in addition to your larger chessboard. Use one set to play the moves of the game and the other to play the variations discussed. In this way you won't lose your place.

An important thing to remember is that once you know the rules, you should take every opportunity to play, whether you win or lose. With practice and study of this book, you will know why you won, or lost, and will find that chess is not only a pleasureable game, but an easy one.

BEATRICE REINFELD

New York, March 1, 1971

LESSON 1: THE ELEMENTS

In a game of chess there are two opponents who take turns making moves. One of them ("White") has the white pieces. The other player ("Black") has the black pieces. White always moves first at the beginning of the game.

Diagram 1

The Chessboard

There are eight horizontal rows, known as "ranks," and eight vertical rows, known as "files." All sixty-four squares are used in the game. Note the white square is always at the lower, right corner.

Diagram 2

The Opening Position

This is how the forces are placed to start the game. Each player has sixteen chessmen as the game begins.

The Elements ■ 11

You will have noticed that there are six different kinds of chessmen shown in Diagram 2. Here are their names:

Here are two important things to keep in mind when you set up the chessmen to begin a game:

(1) The right-hand corner square nearest to White must be a white square.

(2) The two Queens must face each other along the same file, with the White Queen on a white square and the Black Queen on a black square (see Diagram 2). The Kings will also face each other on another file.

The King Bishop is placed on the King Bishop file, next to the King.

The King Knight is placed on the King Knight file, next to the King Bishop.

The King Rook is placed on the King Rook file, next to the King Knight.

The Queen Bishop, Queen Knight and Queen Rook get their names in the same way.

As for the Pawns, each one is named for the piece in front of which it stands on the second rank. Example: the Pawn in front of the Queen is the Queen Pawn.

How the Chessmen Move

Each of the chessmen has a different way of moving. This variety adds a great deal to the charm of chess, and allows the chessmen to co-operate to produce stunning effects.

THE KING

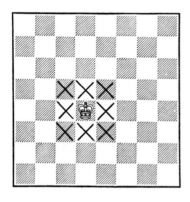

Diagram 3
How the King moves

The King can move one square in any direction—vertically, horizontally and diagonally to any of the squares marked with a cross. A diagonal is a row of squares of the same color all extending in the same direction.

Diagram 4
How the King captures

The King can capture any hostile chessman on an adjacent square. The King captures by displacement. In Diagram 4 the King can capture the Bishop but not the Pawn.

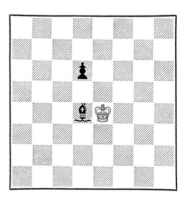

THE QUEEN

The Queen, like the King, can move in any direction. But there is a very important difference—the Queen can keep right on moving until she is blocked by some obstacle to her further progress, such as a friendly chessman. The Queen captures by displacing the hostile chessman it is eliminating.

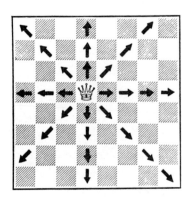

Diagram 5
How the Queen moves

The Queen can move to any square marked with an arrow. As you can see, the Queen has enormous powers, and you will not be surprised to learn that she is the most powerful piece on the board.

Diagram 6
How the Queen captures

The Queen can capture any one of the three Black chessmen. She can capture the Knight (along the rank); or the Black Bishop (along the file); or the Pawn (along the diagonal).

THE ROOK

The Rook moves vertically or horizontally, one direction at a time. It is the second most powerful piece on the board.

The Rook can, within its moving range, capture any hostile chessman (see Diagram 8). The Rook captures by displacing the hostile chessman it is eliminating. The presence of a friendly chessman along a Rook's line of movement makes it impossible for the Rook to move any further along that line.

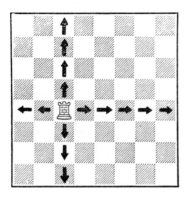

Diagram 7
How the Rook moves

The Rook can move to any square marked with an arrow. As you can see, the number of squares available to the Rook is much smaller than the number available to the Queen.

Diagram 8
How the Rook captures

The Rook can capture the Bishop (horizontal move). Or it can capture the Knight (vertical move). But the Rook cannot *capture the Pawn (diagonal move).*

The Queen and the Rook ■ 15

THE BISHOP

The Bishop moves diagonally, one direction at a time. It is not quite so strong as the Rook.

The Bishop can capture any hostile chessman placed within its moving range (see Diagram 10). The Bishop captures by displacement of the hostile chessman which it is eliminating. The presence of a friendly chessman along a Bishop's line of movement makes it impossible for the Bishop to move any further along that line.

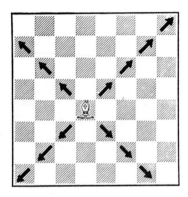

Diagram 9
How the Bishop moves

The Bishop can move to any square marked with an arrow. A Bishop has its greatest scope when placed in the center.

Diagram 10
How the Bishop captures

The Bishop can capture the Rook or the Pawn. The Bishop **cannot** *capture the Knight, however, because the Pawn is in the way.*

THE KNIGHT

The Knight's powers are unique in several respects. For example, the Knight is the only piece that can leap over any other chessman. The Knight, unlike the Queen, Rook, or Bishop, has a move of uniform length. Its move is three squares long, and it can take the following forms:

(1) One square forward or backward; then two squares to the right or left.

(2) One square to the right or left; then two squares forward or backward.

These possibilities are shown in Diagrams 11 and 12.

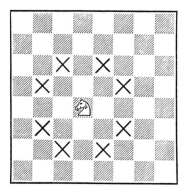

Diagram 11
How the Knight moves

The Knight can move to any one of the squares marked with a cross.

Diagram 12
A typical Knight move

The Knight has made one of the moves indicated in Diagram 11.

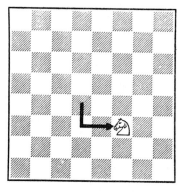

The Knight can capture only on the end-square of its move, displacing the captured chessmen. The Knight cannot capture

The Bishop and the Knight ■ 17

any chessman that it leaps over. These points are illustrated in Diagrams 13 and 14.

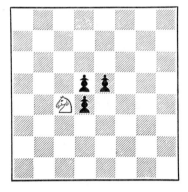

Diagram 13
How the Knight captures

The Knight can capture only one of these Pawns—namely, the Pawn on the end-square of the Knight's move. The other Pawns are safe from capture.

Diagram 14
The completed Knight capture

This is the position that results from the only possible Knight capture in Diagram 13. The Knight can never capture the men it leaps over.

In mastering the Knight's move, you will find it a big help to remember this feature: every time a Knight moves, it changes the color of its square. Starting from a white square, it ends up on a black square. On the other hand, if it starts on a black square, it ends on a white square. (Verify this in Diagrams 11 and 12.)

THE PAWN

The Pawn is the only chessman that can move in only one direction. A White Pawn moves toward the Black side only (Diagrams 15 and 16). A Black Pawn moves toward the White side only (Diagrams 17 and 18). The Pawn moves one square straight ahead unless that square is already occupied by a hostile or friendly man.

Diagram 15

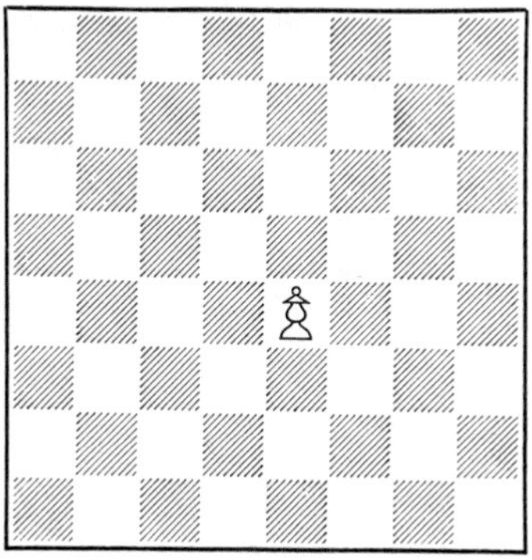

Diagram 16

The White Pawn moves straight ahead.

The White Pawn has completed its move.

Diagram 17

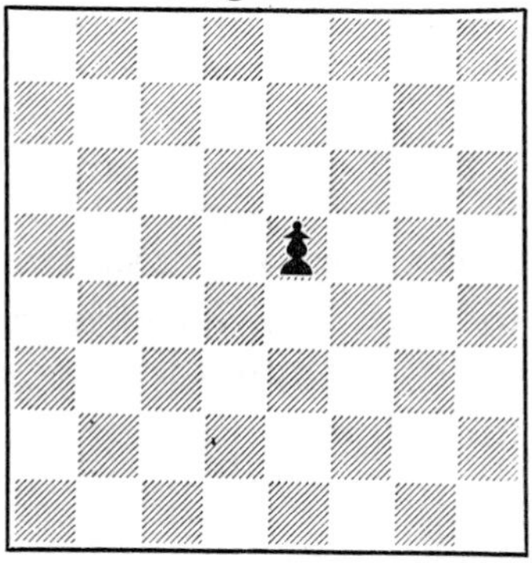

Diagram 18

The Black Pawn moves straight ahead.

The Black Pawn has completed its move.

The Knight and the Pawn ■ 19

The Pawn has an important option. Each Pawn on its first move—not necessarily the first move in the game—has the choice of advancing one square or two squares. These possibilities are illustrated in Diagrams 19 and 20. For unusual powers of the Pawn see Diagrams 55 to 57.

Diagram 19

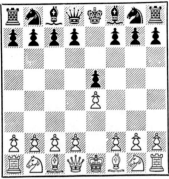

Each King Pawn has advanced two squares.

Diagram 20

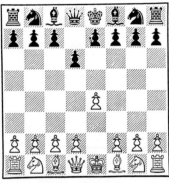

Here Black's Queen Pawn has moved one square; White's Pawn has moved two squares.

A peculiarity of the Pawn is that, unlike any other chessmen, its capturing method differs from the way it moves. A Pawn captures any hostile unit that is diagonally in front of it, to the left or right.

Diagram 21
No capture possible

Neither Pawn can capture the other. The Pawns merely block each other.

20 ■ Lesson 1—The Elements

Diagram 22
A choice of captures

The White Pawn can capture the Black Queen or the Black Knight.

Diagram 23

The Pawn can capture the Bishop.

Diagram 24

The Pawn has captured the Bishop.

Practice how each piece moves and captures on your own board before continuing to the next section.

Check and Checkmate

Though the King is not the strongest piece in chess, it is the most important piece.

Basically, you win a game of chess by attacking the hostile King until it has no escape from capture. Such a situation is known as "Checkmate." (Actually the King is never captured; the fact that the King is attacked and cannot escape is what establishes checkmate.)

An attack on the King is called a "check." If the King can escape from attack, he does so, and the game goes on. If he cannot escape from attack, then he is checkmated, and the game is over. The player who has brought about the checkmate has won the game.

There are three ways of getting out of check:

(1) Capture the hostile man that is giving check.

(2) Move the King off the line of attack. Naturally, you are not permitted to move the King to a square commanded by some other hostile man.

(3) Place one of your own men on the line of attack between your King and the hostile man that is giving check. This is called interposing.

These methods are illustrated in Diagrams 25 to 28.

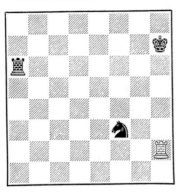

Diagram 25

White's Rook is giving check. Black's King is in check.

Diagram 26

Black is out of check. The Black Knight has captured the White Rook.

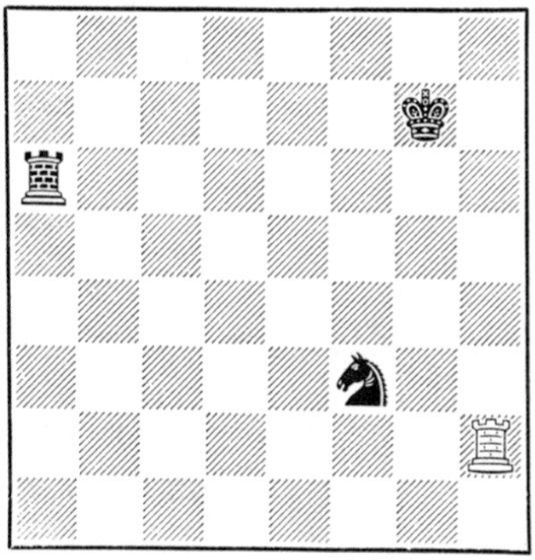

Diagram 27

Black is out of check. Black has moved his King off the line of attack. This is the second method.

Diagram 28

Black is out of check. Black has interposed his Rook on the line of attack. This is the third method.

To understand the nature of checkmate, you must keep in mind that a King can never move to a square which is in the capturing range of a hostile man.

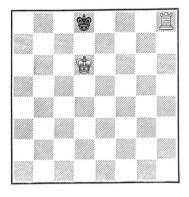

Diagram 29
Black is checkmated

White's Rook is checking the Black King. Horizontal King moves are useless, as the King remains on the line of attack. Other King moves are impossible as they would bring the Black King inside the capturing range of the White King. Finally, White's Rook cannot be captured.

Diagram 30
White is checkmated

Black's Knight is checking White's King. White cannot capture the Knight. White cannot interpose (one can never interpose to a Knight check). And the White King cannot move into the Black Bishop's capturing range.

DISCOVERED CHECK

Generally a piece gives check by moving to the proper square for that purpose. In the case of a discovered ("uncovered") check, the checking piece stands still while one of its colleagues moves off the line of attack, allowing the hitherto hidden piece to give check.

This is illustrated in Diagram 31, where White's Queen need not move to give check. This is accomplished by advancing the Pawn.

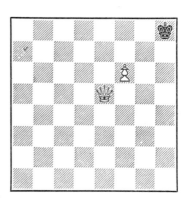

Diagram 31
The Pawn will advance

White moves his Pawn in order to give a discovered check with his Queen, which remains unmoved.

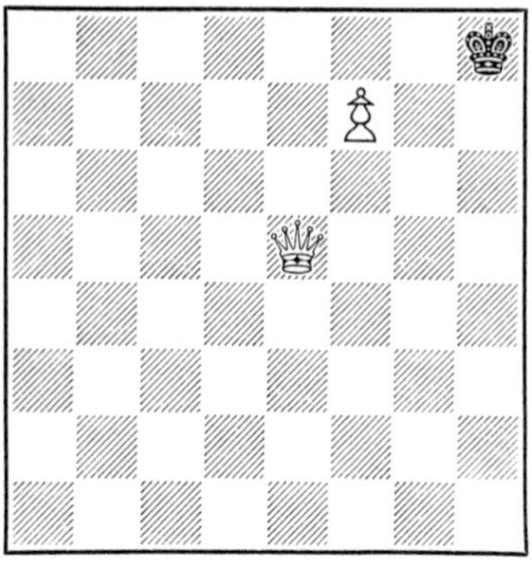

Diagram 32
Discovered check

Black's King is in check, despite the fact that the White Queen has not moved.

DOUBLE CHECK

The double check is a special and particularly formidable kind of discovered check.

What happens in a double check is that the piece that uncovers the line of attack also gives check as it moves off. Thus in Diagram 33 the Bishop will move and open up the Queen's line of attack. But in addition, the Bishop itself will also give check.

In the case of a simple discovered check, the defender theoretically has the choice of the three possible ways of answering a check—capturing the checking man, moving the King out of check, or interposing on the line of attack. Against a double check, there is only one possible defense—moving the King out of both lines of attack.

Diagram 33

The Bishop will move

White will move his Bishop to open the Queen's line of attack. But the Bishop will also give check.

Diagram 34

Double Check

Both White's Queen and his Bishop are giving check. Black cannot capture the Bishop or Queen.

Castling

We have learned that the outcome of a game of chess centers about the fate of the King. We saw that the King himself does not have very much power. This all-important piece therefore requires the most careful shielding to keep it out of harm's way.

One of the most effective devices to guard the King's safety is the process known as "castling." This is a special move performed by the King and a Rook. It can be played only once during the course of a game, and it is the only move in chess in which two different pieces take part—with both moves counting as a single move. Castling with the King Rook is known as "King-side castling." Castling with the Queen Rook is "Queen-side castling."

One basic requirement for castling is that the squares between the King and his castling Rook are empty.

KING-SIDE CASTLING

In King-side castling (Diagram 35), White moves his King two squares to the right. He then places his King Rook directly to the left of the King's new position (Diagram 36).

Diagram 35	**Diagram 36**

Before King-side castling. White is about to castle. *After King-side castling. White has castled.*

Double Check and Castling ■ 27

Diagram 37	Diagram 38

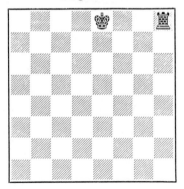 

Before King-side castling. Black is about to castle.   *After King-side castling. Black has castled.*

As for Black (Diagram 37), he moves his King two squares to his left. He then places his King Rook directly to the right of the King's new position (Diagram 38).

QUEEN-SIDE CASTLING

To castle on the Queen-side (Diagram 39), White moves his King two squares to the left. He then places his Queen Rook directly to the right of his King's new position (Diagram 40).

Diagram 39	Diagram 40

Before Queen-side castling. White is about to castle.   *After Queen-side castling. White has castled.*

When Black castles on the Queen-side (Diagram 41) he moves his King two squares to his right. He then places his Queen Rook directly to the left of his King's new position (Diagram 42).

Diagram 41

Before Queen-side castling.
Black is about to castle.

Diagram 42

After Queen-side castling.
Black has castled.

RESTRICTIONS ON CASTLING

There are two kinds of restrictions on castling; some of these hold good for the whole game, while others may not apply later on in the game.

There are two kinds of permanent restrictions. If the King has already moved (Diagram 43), then castling is permanently impossible.

Diagram 43
Black can never castle

Black has moved his King; hence his castling is permanently barred.

Castling ■ 29

If the Rook desired for castling has already moved (Diagram 44), castling with that Rook is impossible.

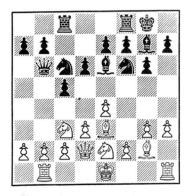

Diagram 44
White cannot castle Queen-side

However, he can castle with his unmoved King Rook.

Now we turn to the castling restrictions that are temporary. By this we mean that if the restrictive condition disappears, it will then be possible to castle.

Castling is temporarily impossible if all the squares between King and Rook are not vacant (Diagram 45).

Diagram 45

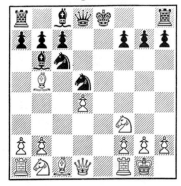

Black is temporarily unable to castle Queen-side. He can, however, castle King-side if he wishes.

Diagram 46

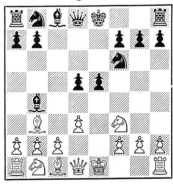

White is temporarily unable to castle because his King is in check.

Castling is temporarily impossible for a King that is in check (Diagram 46). If the King gets out of check without moving, castling will then become feasible.

Castling is temporarily impossible if a King, in order to castle, would have to pass over a square controlled by an enemy unit (Diagram 47).

And of course, castling is temporarily impossible if it would land the King on a square controlled by an enemy unit (Diagram 48).

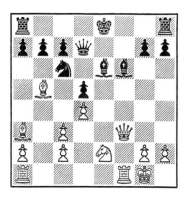

Diagram 47
Black is temporarily unable to castle on the King-side

The black square over which the King has to pass is controlled by the White Queen Bishop.

Diagram 48
White is temporarily unable to castle

Castling would land his King on a square commanded by Black's King Bishop.

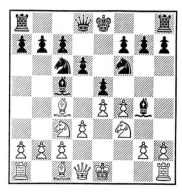

You now know all the elements of the game, and you are ready to learn how to value your pieces in the next lesson.

LESSON 2: BEGINNING YOUR CHESS STUDY

Each unit on the chessboard has a value which is different from the values of other units. How can you know whether you are giving up a more valuable unit in return for capturing a less valuable one? Or, how can you know whether you are gaining a hostile unit of greater value than the unit you are giving up in exchange?

There is a common-sense solution to this problem. The Pawn is the least valuable of all the various units, so we give it an arbitrary value. Then we express the values of the other units in terms of that value.

So, to begin with, we say the Pawn is worth one point. This gives us the following table of values:

Queen	9 points
Rook	5 points
Bishop	3 points
Knight	3 points
Pawn	1 point

We cannot assign any value to the King since the outcome of the game hinges on his preservation!

When we study this table we can derive some valuable conclusions:

The Queen is the strongest and most valuable of the pieces (always excepting the King, of course).

A Bishop and a Knight are of equal value. This means you

can readily give up a Bishop in exchange for a hostile Knight; or you can give up a Knight in exchange for a hostile Bishop.

A Rook is definitely worth more than a Bishop or Knight. Winning your opponent's Rook in return for a "minor piece" (Bishop or Knight of your own) is known as "winning *the* Exchange." Losing your Rook in return for a hostile minor piece is "losing *the* Exchange."

A minor piece plus two Pawns are roughly the equivalent of a Rook.

A Rook and two Pawns are roughly the equivalent of two minor pieces.

The Pawn is the least valuable of the units—but don't despise the "lowly" Pawn. There are special situations in which you can convert a Pawn into a Queen. This is our next subject to be discussed.

Other Powers of the Pawn

In the original treatment of the Pawn's powers, two points were left for later discussion. Let us take them up at this time.

PAWN PROMOTION

When a Pawn reaches the eighth rank—that is to say, the last square in a file—it is promoted to a higher rank. It can and must be converted into a Queen or Rook or Bishop or Knight at the player's option. Generally a new Queen is his choice, as this piece is the strongest on the board, but there is no limitation on the player's choice. For example, even if he still has his original Queen he is not debarred from promoting to a second Queen.

The advance of a Pawn to the eighth rank and its replacement by a new piece of the same color are all considered to comprise a single move. Thereafter the newly promoted piece must wait for the opponent's reply before making its first move.

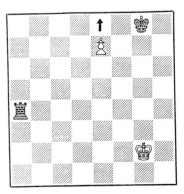

Diagram 50 ———→
The new Queen in action

White's new Queen gives
check and also attacks Black's
Rook, winning the Rook next
move.

Diagram 49
White promotes his Pawn

White advances his Pawn to
the eighth rank, replacing it
with a White Queen.

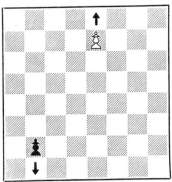

Diagram 51
Both players obtain new Queens

First White advances his
Pawn and obtains a new
Queen. The Black advances
his Pawn and likewise obtains
a new Queen.

Diagram 52
Both players have new Queens

Each player has advanced a
Pawn to the last rank and
obtained a new Queen. Note
that the Pawns "queen" at
opposite ends of the board.

Diagram 53
Black's King must move

*It is Black's turn to move
and his Pawns are blocked.
In moving, Black can no
longer guard his Bishop
Pawn. His King retreats, and
the Pawn falls.*

Diagram 54
Black loses his last Pawn

*White will capture the Black
Pawn. His own Pawn will then
be free to advance.*

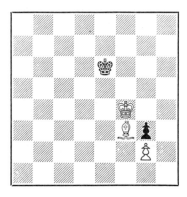

It is not surprising that the queening of a Pawn is often the means of winning a game. Suppose that in the position of Diagram 53 White had no Pawn left. In that case he could not win, as King and Bishop cannot force checkmate. However, as matters stand, he can win the Black Pawns, after which his remaining Pawn, escorted by King and Bishop, advances to the queening square. Then, having obtained a new Queen, he forces checkmate quickly and easily. Thus the seemingly insignificant Pawn is the key to victory.

Very often when one of the players has obtained a considerable advantage ("plus") in material and checkmate is a foregone conclusion, his opponent will resign—concede defeat—instead of playing out the dismal interval that will elapse before checkmate takes place.

PAWN CAPTURES EN PASSANT ("IN PASSING")

This is an unusual form of capture which is possible only when four specific conditions exist:

(1) The Pawn that does the capturing must be on its fifth rank.

(2) The hostile Pawn that is destined to be captured must be on an adjacent file and on its original rank (Diagram 55).

(3) It is the opponent's turn to move and he advances his Pawn two squares (Diagram 56).

(4) The hostile Pawn, having advanced two squares, can be captured as if it had advanced only one square (Diagram 57).

Diagram 55
En passant capture

First stage: the Pawns are on adjacent files. One Pawn is on its fifth rank, the other Pawn is on its second rank.

Diagram 56
En passant capture

Second stage: the Black Pawn advances two squares.

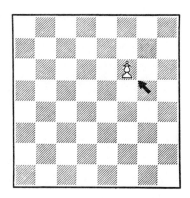

Diagram 57
En passant capture

Final stage: the White Pawn captures the Black Pawn en passant.

While capturing in passing is purely optional, the capture, if it is to be played at all, must come on the immediate reply to the two-square advance of the hostile Pawn. If not exercised at once, the option lapses.

If capturing in passing is the only way to answer a check to one's King, then the capture is compulsory. On the other hand, if capturing in passing would expose one's King to attack, then such capture is impossible.

How to Read Chess Moves

There are several systems for recording chess moves. They are all based on the same principle: each chessman and each square must have a definite name. These names are derived from the opening position (Diagram 58).

(See next page)

Diagram 58

The opening position

Diagram 59

The Files

QUEEN-ROOK'S FILE	QUEEN-KNIGHT'S FILE	QUEEN-BISHOP'S FILE	QUEEN'S FILE	KING'S FILE	KING-BISHOP'S FILE	KING-KNIGHT'S FILE	KING-ROOK'S FILE

The Files

The names of the pieces, reading from left to right, appear below. The Pawns get their names from the pieces in front of which they are placed (for example, Queen Pawn in front of the Queen, etc.). Note the abbreviations commonly used.

The files are named for the pieces (and the accompanying Pawns) that are placed on them at the beginning of the game. These names are permanent, even though the position of the identifying pieces and Pawns will change during the game.

Names of the Pieces

Queen Rook (QR)
Queen Knight (QN)
Queen Bishop (QB)
Queen (Q)
King (K)
King Bishop (KB)
King Knight (KN)
King Rook (KR)

Names of the Corresponding Pawns

Queen Rook Pawn (QRP)
Queen Knight Pawn (QNP)
Queen Bishop Pawn (QBP)
Queen Pawn (QP)
King Pawn (KP)
King Bishop Pawn (KBP)
King Knight Pawn (KNP)
King Rook Pawn (KRP)

The ranks are the horizontal rows that are numbered by each player from *his* side of the board (Diagrams 60 and 61).

Diagram 60

8 WHITE'S EIGHTH RANK
7
6
5
4
3
2
1 WHITE'S   FIRST   RANK

The ranks from White's side

Diagram 61

1 BLACK'S   FIRST   RANK
2
3
4
5
6
7
8 BLACK'S EIGHTH RANK

The ranks from Black's side

The recording of White's moves is based on his numbering of the ranks as shown above.

The recording of Black's moves is based on his numbering of the ranks as shown above.

Now that we know the names of all the files (Diagram 59) and the numbers of all the ranks (Diagrams 60 and 61), we have all the information we need for recording moves.

Here is the most important point to remember: each rank has two numbers—White's number and Black's number. In Diagram 61 White's second rank becomes Black's seventh rank, for example. Also, you can see that each square has to have two names—one from White's side of the board and one from Black's side of the board.

Now when White is recording his moves, he uses the White numbering of the ranks (Diagram 60). When Black is recording *his* moves, he uses the Black numbering of the ranks.

As you can see from Diagram 62, the name of any square is a combination of the file and rank on which it stands. For example, the square on which the King stands is King 1 (K1), or first square on the King file. The square on which the King Pawn stands is King 2 (K2), or the second square in the King file.

BLACK

QR1 / QR8	QN1 / QN8	QB1 / QB8	Q1 / Q8	K1 / K8	KB1 / KB8	KN1 / KN8	KR1 / KR8
QR2 / QR7	QN2 / QN7	QB2 / QB7	Q2 / Q7	K2 / K7	KB2 / KB7	KN2 / KN7	KR2 / KR7
QR3 / QR6	QN3 / QN6	QB3 / QB6	Q3 / Q6	K3 / K6	KB3 / KB6	KN3 / KN6	KR3 / KR6
QR4 / QR5	QN4 / QN5	QB4 / QB5	Q4 / Q5	K4 / K5	KB4 / KB5	KN4 / KN5	KR4 / KR5
QR5 / QR4	QN5 / QN4	QB5 / QB4	Q5 / Q4	K5 / K4	KB5 / KB4	KN5 / KN4	KR5 / KR4
QR6 / QR3	QN6 / QN3	QB6 / QB3	Q6 / Q3	K6 / K3	KB6 / KB3	KN6 / KN3	KR6 / KR3
QR7 / QR2	QN7 / QN2	QB7 / QB2	Q7 / Q2	K7 / K2	KB7 / KB2	KN7 / KN2	KR7 / KR2
QR8 / QR1	QN8 / QN1	QB8 / QB1	Q8 / Q1	K8 / K1	KB8 / KB1	KN8 / KN1	KR8 / KR1

WHITE

Diagram 62

The names of the squares

In Diagram 62 the name at the bottom of each square is White's name for that square and it is used to record White moves. The upside-down name of each square is Black's name for that square, and is used to record Black moves.

To record a move, we write down the name of the unit that is making the move, add a dash and then the name of the square to which it has moved. For example, if White moves his King Pawn two squares he writes, "P—K4". If Black replies by advancing *his* King Pawn two squares he also writes, "P—K4". (This gives us the position of Diagram 63.)

In an ordinary game score (also known as the "text" of the game), the moves are listed in two columns, with White's moves in the left column and Black's moves in the right column. In addition the moves are numbered, so that you can follow the correct order of the moves.

To save time, we use abbreviations and short-cut symbols for the moves. Here are the most important ones:

King	K	discovered check	dis ch
Queen	Q	double check	dbl ch
Rook	R	*en passant* (in passing)	*e.p.*
Bishop	B	Castles King-side	O—O
Knight	N	Castles Queen-side	O—O—O
Pawn	P	a good move	!
captures	×	a very good move	!!
moves to	—	a bad move	?
check	ch	a very bad move	??
		from or at	/

Here are some examples of abbreviation: N—KB3 means "Knight moves to King Bishop three." Q×B means "Queen takes Bishop." R—K8 ch means "Rook moves to King eight giving check."

A SAMPLE GAME

If you are eager to become a good player—and who isn't?—you will benefit enormously from studying chess books. It is easy to do once you are familiar with the recording of chess moves. Here is a short, instructive game which has the additional virtue of illustrating dynamic winning tactics.

	WHITE	BLACK
1	P—K4	P—K4
2	N—KB3	N—KB3
3	N×P	N—B3
4	N×N	QP×N
5	P—Q3	B—QB4
6	B—N5	N×P!!
7	B×Q	B×Pch
8	K—K2	B—KN5 mate

Since the recording of moves is still a novel experience to you, we will follow the course of the game in slow motion through a detailed series of diagrams. To begin, set up the forces on your chessboard in the opening position (Diagram 58) and make each recorded move. If any of the moves puzzle you, consult Diagram 62 for the names of the squares.

The game starts with White playing 1 P—K4 and Black replying 1 . . . P—K4. This gives us the situation in Diagram 63.

Diagram 63

	WHITE	BLACK
2	N—KB3	N—KB3
3	N×P	N—B3
4	N×N	QP×N

See Diagram 64.

Diagram 64

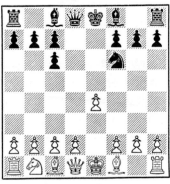

Play continues:

	WHITE	BLACK
5	P—Q3	B—QB4
6	B—N5	N×P!!

On the face of it, a terrible blunder.

See Diagram 65.

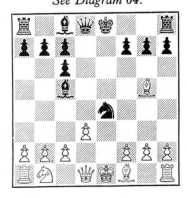

⟵ **Diagram 65**

Play continues:

	WHITE	BLACK
7	B×Q	B×Pch
8	K—K2	B—KN5mate

See Diagram 66.

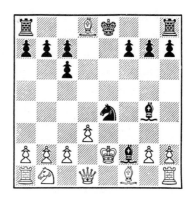

Diagram 66
Final position:

White's King has no escape.
Black's brilliant Queen
sacrifice resulted in a very
quick checkmate.

We have seen that the basic method of winning a game of chess is to checkmate the opposing King. A common way of leading up to this is to gain material—to win your opponent's pieces or to capture more valuable ones in exchange for less valuable pieces of your own. Another way of leading up to victory is to promote one of your Pawns to a new Queen. Very often when one player is considerably ahead in material, his outnumbered opponent simply "resigns"—he formally admits defeat. The game is over, just as if he had been checkmated. Not all games, however, end with checkmate or resignation. Some are "drawn"—they end with victory for neither side.

Drawn Games

A draw is a game which ends with honors even—each side scores a half-point. Here are the ways in which such a result may come about.

DRAWING METHODS

A draw can be declared by mutual agreement of the players.
Either player can claim a draw if fifty moves have been made by each player without a capture or Pawn move having been made. (This is likely to arise only at a very advanced, highly simplified stage of the game.)

A player can claim a draw if he is on the point of making a move that would result for the third time in the same position.

There are other drawing possibilities that require more detailed description.

INADEQUATE CHECKMATING MATERIAL

A player may be ahead in material but his margin of advantage may not be enough to force checkmate. It is impossible, for example, to force checkmate in endings with King and Bishop against King, or King and Knight against King (See Diagram 67), or even with King and two Knights against King.

Diagram 67
Drawn position

White's King can never be cornered, as some means of escape will always be available. The ending of King and Bishop against King is equally futile.

Diagram 68
Perpetual check

	WHITE	BLACK
1	Q—K8ch	K—R2
2	Q—R5ch	K—N1
3	Q—K8ch	K—R2
4	Q—R5ch etc.	

DRAW BY PERPETUAL CHECK

This self-explanatory term applies to situations in which a player has the power to give an endless series of checks. It is a device that makes it possible to convert an otherwise surely lost game into a forced draw. See Diagram 68, in which White, although he is a long way behind in material, is able to force a draw.

DRAW BY STALEMATE

This method of causing a drawn game has to be distinguished very carefully from checkmate. In the case of checkmate, the King is attacked (in check) and has no legal move.

Diagram 69
Stalemate

Black (to move) is stalemated. Any move of the Black King would bring him inside the capturing range of White's Queen.

Diagram 70
Stalemate

Black (to move) is stalemated. His Pawn cannot move and any move of his King would bring him inside the capturing range of White's King or Knight.

Draws and Stalemates ■ 45

In the case of stalemate, the following conditions have to be fulfilled:

(1) The player who claims stalemate has to be on the move.

(2) His King must *not* be in check.

(3) The only moves left to him would place his King inside the capturing range of some hostile unit.

You now know enough to be able to sit down at a chessboard with a friend and play. But you need a great deal more information to be able to win.

Before you go on to the next lesson, return to page 41 and play over the same game until you are thoroughly familiar with chess notation. Then play through the positions and moves of the next chapter once without great depth of thought. You will learn a little. The next time you play through, you will learn more. Finally, you will see all of the points to be made. You will recognize checkmate patterns, threats, checks, pins and forks. Give plenty of time to Lesson 3.

LESSON 3:
WINNING OBJECTIVES
AND METHODS

Forcing checkmate is always our basic goal in a game of chess. Meanwhile, our immediate aims are: winning material; checks; Pawn promotion; and threats. Each of these may be a step on the way to checkmate.

CHECKMATE PATTERNS

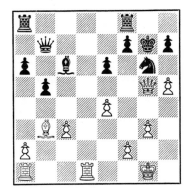

Diagram 71
Mate on King Knight 7

White to move. Ordinarily White's proper play would be P×N. *Here, however, he has a stronger move:*

WHITE	BLACK
1 P—R6ch!	K moves
2 Q—B6	......

Black is helpless against 3 Q—N7 mate.

Diagram 72
Mate on the long diagonal

Black to move. Based on the power of his Bishop on the long diagonal, this brilliant sacrifice is conclusive:

WHITE	BLACK
1	R×P!
2 K×R	Q—R3ch
3 K—N1	Q—R8 mate

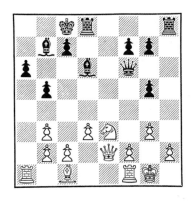

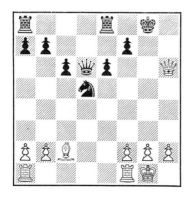

Diagram 73

*Mating attack against King
Rook 7*

White to move.

	WHITE	BLACK
1	B—R7ch	K—R1
2	B—N6 dis ch!	K—N1
3	Q—R7ch	K—B1
4	Q×P mate	

*This is a very common form of
attack, with many
applications in actual play.*

Diagram 74
Smothered mate

White to move.

	WHITE	BLACK
1	Q—Q5ch	K—R1

*(or 1. . . . . . K—B1; and then
2 Q—B7 mate.)*

2	N—B7ch	K—N1
3	N—R6 dbl ch!	K—R1
4	Q—N8ch!!	R×Q
5	N—B7 mate	

*This spectacular mating
technique leads to a pleasing
finish.*

CHECKMATE THREATS CAN WIN MATERIAL

Even if your opponent can parry it, a checkmate threat may still lead to decisive material gains. Diagrams 75 and 76 illustrate the point effectively.

Diagram 75
Checkmate menace

White to move.

WHITE	BLACK
1 Q—B5!	......

White threatens Q×RPch followed by Q—R8 mate, and he attacks Black's Rook at the same time.

| 1 ...... | P—N3 |

Black can stop the mate but he cannot save his Rook.

2 Q×Rch and wins.

Diagram 76
Checkmate menace

White to move.

WHITE	BLACK
1 Q—Q4!	......

White threatens Q—N7 mate or Q—R8 mate and attacks Black's Knight at Queen Rook 7 as well.

| 1 ...... | P—B3 |

Black stops the mate but he cannot parry the other threat.

2 Q×N/R7 and wins.

Checkmate Threats ■ 49

CHECKS WIN MATERIAL

Many a check has a secondary purpose—to attack another unit in addition to the hostile King. This is shown in Diagrams 77 and 78.

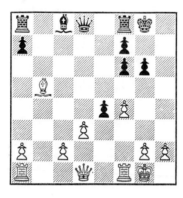

Diagram 77
A versatile check

Black to move.

WHITE	BLACK
1	Q—N3ch

This check wins White's Bishop, as White must concentrate on getting out of check. This kind of double attack *occurs very frequently.*

Diagram 78
Two versatile checks

White to move.

WHITE	BLACK
1 R—Q7ch	R—B2

Else White captures the Bishop.

2 R×Rch	K×R
3 B—B8 dis ch	......

White wins the Bishop.

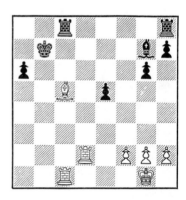

PAWN PROMOTION WINS MATERIAL

The conversion of a Pawn into a unit of higher value, when successfully executed, will often win material. See Diagrams 79 and 80.

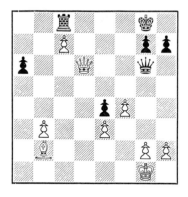

Diagram 79

The Queen Bishop Pawn queens

White to move.

WHITE	BLACK
1 Q—Q7!	R—B1

If Black defends the attacked Rook with 1 ...... Q—K1 White replies 2 Q×P mate.

| 2 P—B8/Q | R×Q |

Black has no choice.

3   Q×Rch and wins.

Diagram 80

The Queen Knight Pawn queens

White to move.

WHITE	BLACK
1	R—R8

Black threatens 2 ...... R×R; 3 Q×R, P—N8/Q with a whole Queen ahead.

| 2 R—N1 | R×R |
| 3 Q×R | N—B6 and wins. |

Black gets a new Queen.

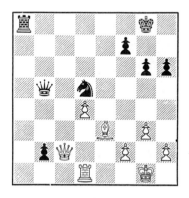

Winning Material ■ 51

THREATS WIN MATERIAL

There are many kinds of threats which win material because your opponent cannot defend himself against every possibility. The point is effectively made in Diagrams 81 and 82.

Diagram 81

Black wins by a double attack

Black to move.

WHITE	BLACK
1	P×P!

This is really a triple attack! The Pawn capture attacks White's Queen and Bishop— and also his advanced Knight as well.

| 2 B×BP | B×Nch! |

Here 2 ...... Q×N? is wrong because of 3 Q×B.

| 3 P×B | Q×N and wins. |

Diagram 82

The Queen Bishop Pawn is the target

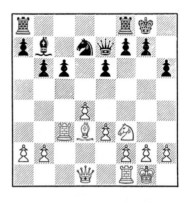

White to move.

WHITE	BLACK
1 B—K4!	KR—B1

White threatened 2 B×P. Now he simply keeps renewing the threat.

2 Q—B2	Q—Q3
3 KR—B1	N—N1
4 N—K5	......

This finally wins the Queen Bishop Pawn, as Black has run out of defensive resources.

Winning Methods

As we have seen in the previous section, it is important to know our basic winning objectives. But this is not the whole story: we also have to be familiar with winning techniques and able to recognize winning possibilities.

EXPOSED KING

This is one of the best guides we have for the progress of a winning attack. Sometimes the hostile King is approachable through a line of attack, or because he is not securely guarded by his pieces. See Diagrams 83 and 84.

Diagram 83	Diagram 84

A deadly discovered check	*Unavoidable mate*

White to move. The presence of Black's King on an open file proves fatal.

WHITE	BLACK
1 N—B5 dis ch	......

Thanks to the exposed position of Black's King, White wins his Queen for a mere Knight.

White to move. Black's King Knight Pawn has captured on his King Bishop 3, opening up a gaping hole in his castled position. Therefore:

WHITE	BLACK
1 Q—R6	......

Black cannot prevent Q—N7 mate.

OPEN LINES

Open lines enormously increase the mobility of your forces, making it possible for them to maneuver more effectively. And when one or more of these open lines lead to the vicinity of the hostile King, it may well be that you have the makings of a violent, quickly decisive attack. See Diagrams 85 and 86.

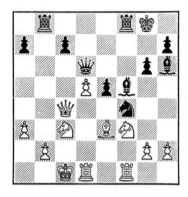

Diagram 85
The open Queen Knight file

Black to move. Black wins on the spot with:

WHITE	BLACK
1	Q—N3!!

This threatens ...... Q×P mate and also ..... Q×Bch.

| 2 B×Q | N—K7 mate |

A deadly double check.

Diagram 86
The open King Rook file

White to move. The open file is White's highway to victory. In fact, he has a forced mate.

WHITE	BLACK
1 R—R8ch	K—B2
2 Q×Nch!	K×Q
3 R/R1—R7 mate	

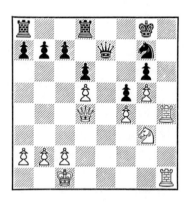

PREPONDERANCE OF PIECES

If you have more attacking units than your opponent has available for defense, you will succeed in your aim whatever it may be, but even material equality becomes unimportant when you possess a concentration of force on a vulnerable point. See Diagrams 87 and 88.

Diagram 87
Windmill checks

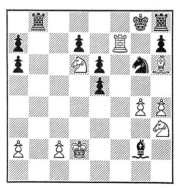

White to move. The co-operation of his Rook, Bishop and Knight is something to marvel at.

WHITE	BLACK
1 R—N7ch	K—B1
2 R×QP dis ch	K—N1
3 R—KN7 ch	K—B1
4 R—QN7 dis ch	K—N1
5 R×Rch	N—B1
6 R×N mate	

Diagram 88
Queen sacrifice

Black to move. He can bring a heavy concentration of forces to bear on the hostile King, while White's forces are shut off from the defense.

WHITE	BLACK
1	Q×RPch!!

Beautiful play.

WHITE	BLACK
2 K×Q	R—R3ch
3 K—N3	R—R6 mate

Winning Methods ■ 55

THE FORK

This simultaneous attack on two hostile units is perhaps the deadliest attack in chess. When this attack operates in different directions, it is particularly likely to be overlooked by inexperienced players. This is particularly true of the Knight fork—the most common, and most insidious, of the forks. See Diagrams 89 to 91.

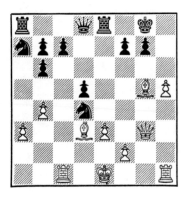

Diagram 89
A Knight fork

Black to move. A sham Queen sacrifice is justified by the resulting Knight fork.

WHITE	BLACK
1	Q×B!
2 Q×Q	N—B6ch

This Knight fork is followed by 3 ...... N×Q, leaving Black a piece ahead.

Diagram 90
Prepared Knight fork

Black to move. He wants to play the deadly forking move ...... N—K7ch, winning White's Queen; but White's Bishop on Queen 3 foils him; so:

WHITE	BLACK
1	R×B!
2 P×R	N—K7ch

Black wins the White Queen.

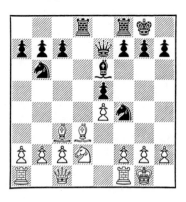

Diagram 91
An elaborately prepared Knight fork

White to move.

	WHITE	BLACK
1	N—Q5!	Q—K3
2	Q×N!	Q×Q
3	N—B6ch	......

White continues with 4 N×Q, remaining with a substantial advantage in material.

Diagram 92
A Pawn fork

White to move. This type of attack is dreaded because the attacker's investment is so small.

	WHITE	BLACK
1	P—K5	......

White attacks two Black pieces, thereby forcing the win of a piece.

THE PIN

This is the most common of all attacking methods in chess. It is an attack on two units standing on a file, rank or diagonal. There is a direct attack on the nearest hostile piece—the pinned piece—on the line of attack. There is a contingent attack on the second hostile unit which is screened from attack by the pinned piece. In Diagram 93, Black's King Bishop Pawn is pinned, as it screens Black's King from attack. In Diagram 94, Black's Knight at his King Bishop 2 is pinned, again screening the Black King from attack.

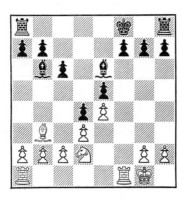

Diagram 93
The pin wins a piece

White to move.

WHITE	BLACK
1 B×B	......

White wins a clear piece, as Black cannot recapture, because his King Bishop Pawn is pinned by White's King Rook. This is a very common pattern.

Diagram 94
The pin leads to mate

White to move.

WHITE	BLACK
1 R×N!	P×R
2 B—R8!	......

Black cannot prevent Q—N7 mate, as ...... K×B or ...... N×B is impossible.

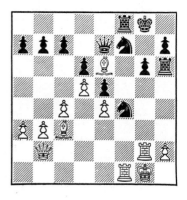

The screened piece is generally one of very high value—King or Queen. (See Diagrams 93 to 96.) When the King is the screened piece—as in Diagram 93—the pinned unit cannot budge; for any such move would expose its King to check. If any piece but the King is being screened, it can be exposed to attack by a move of the pinned unit; but this is undesirable because of the loss of material involved.

Diagram 95
Fork plus pin

Black to move. First he pins White's Queen.

WHITE	BLACK
1	B—KN5!
2 Q×B	N—K6ch!

This Knight fork wins the White Queen because his Queen Pawn is pinned.

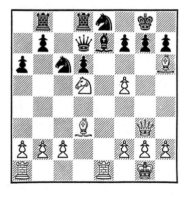

Diagram 96
Fork plus pin

White to move. Note how White exploits his pin on Black's King Knight Pawn.

WHITE	BLACK
1 R×B!	N×R
2 N—B6ch!	N×N
3 Q×NP mate	

Very cleverly played.

DISCOVERED ATTACK

This is another attacking device which is exceptionally strong against inexperienced players. It comprises two simultaneous attacks in this manner: a piece makes a powerful attack without moving, as the result of an uncovering move by one of its colleagues which is likewise following up an aggressive idea.

For example, in Diagram 97, White's Knight at Queen 4 attacks Black's Queen and, in so doing, uncovers an attack by White's Queen on one of the Black Knights. Result: White wins a piece, as Black must save his Queen.

In Diagram 98, White gives check with a Bishop and in the process he uncovers an attack by his Queen on Black's unguarded Queen. Here White wins the Black Queen as Black must get out of check.

Diagram 97

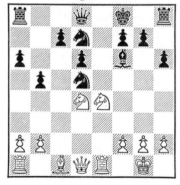

Discovered attack by a White Knight

Diagram 98

Discovered attack by a White Bishop

White to move.

WHITE	BLACK
1 N—B6!	Q moves
2 Q×N and wins	

White to move.

WHITE	BLACK
1 B×Pch!	K×B
2 Q×Q and wins	

UNEXPECTED CAPTURES

The average player constantly overlooks possible captures—either of his own pieces, or the enemy's. Missing these opportunities often leads to disaster. By the same token, taking advantage of them is frequently the way to win. See Diagrams 99 and 100.

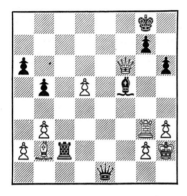

Diagram 99
All is not lost

Black to move. At first glance he seems hopelessly lost because of White's threatened Q×NP mate. Yet, if he is alert, Black can completely turn the tables.

WHITE	BLACK
1	Q×Rch!

White resigns, for now Black's King Knight Pawn is no longer pinned, permitting 2, ... P×Q in reply to 2 K×Q.

Diagram 100
Sudden checkmate

White to move. Obviously White has a very powerful game on the open King Knight file, but how many players could see the following fine finish:

WHITE	BLACK
1 Q×NPch!!	N×Q
2 R×Nch	K—R1
3 R—N8 dbl ch!!	K×R
4 R—KN1ch	Q—N4
5 R×Q mate	

A glorious finish.

DISCOVERED CHECK

An important winning method is use of the *discovered check*. (The word "discovered" is used here in the sense of "uncovered.")

As a rule, a check results when a piece moves into a position to give check. But the discovered check, shown in Diagram 101 operates on a different principle.

In the position of Diagram 101, White's Pawn masks the attack of his Queen on the Black King. By advancing, the Pawn open up the Queen's attack—opens up a discovered check.

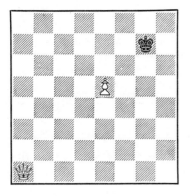

Diagram 101
White to move

By advancing his Pawn, White will enable his Queen to give check.

What makes the discovered check so dangerous (to the defender) is the possibility of a double attack. When a piece moves to uncover a discovered check, it may be attacking some other undefended unit.

In such cases there is no time to defend. *The check must be taken care of first.* (Since checkmate means the loss of the game, you MUST get out of check if at all possible.)

DOUBLE CHECK

Nasty as the discovered check is, it is even nastier if it comes in the form of a *double check*.

Go back for a moment to the position of Diagram 101. Replace the White Pawn with a White Rook. Now have the Rook move to the position it occupies in Diagram 102.

Diagram 102

White gives double check

What happened? The Rook, by moving, has created a discovered check by the Queen. But there is more to it than that. *The Rook is itself giving check!* Thus Black is subjected to double check. His King is checked by the Queen AND the Rook.

To a double check there is only one defense. Interposing a piece won't do, because it is impossible to close both lines of attack. Capturing a checking piece won't do, because the other attacker will still be giving check!

The only solution, then, is to move the King to a spot where he is no longer subject to attack. Sometimes it is possible to get the King to a safe hideaway. Sometimes it isn't—and then the game is lost!

FORKING CHECKS

Still another nasty kind of check is the *forking check*, whereby a Knight attacks the King and another piece at the same time.

This type of check illustrates one of the Knight's most formidable powers. Many a game has been lost when two important pieces were caught on the prongs of a Knight's forking check.

Diagram 103

A forking check

EXPLOITING INFERIOR MOVES

It is the hallmark of a good player that he immediately seizes on hostile weaknesses. Later we shall examine in some detail the ways in which such weaknesses are created. But here we can see the fatal consequences of two types of weak play.

One of these is a substantial loss of time in the opening because of ill-considered Pawn-grabbing expeditions. This is illustrated in Diagram 104, where we have a situation in which White has a significant advantage in open lines and actively functioning pieces. These outweigh by far the two measly Pawns that Black has confiscated.

Diagram 105 illustrates still another faulty type of play in the opening—sending the Queen on distant excursions far from the real scene of action. The punishment is swift and crushing.

Diagram 104
Mobility wins

White to move.

WHITE	BLACK
1 Q×Pch!!	Resigns

For 1 ...... N×Q allows
2 B×P mate.

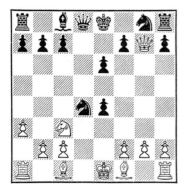

Diagram 105
Checkmate

Black to move.

WHITE	BLACK
1	N×Pch
2 K—K2	Q—Q6 *mate*

White's Queen was missed.

By now you know how to win. This lesson should have taken you no more than four to six hours to read, study and play out. Tomorrow go on to Lesson 4.

LESSON 4: THE OPENINGS AND BASIC CHECKMATES

Your basic task in the opening stage of any game is to bring out pieces—"develop" them. As long as they are on their original squares they are useless. Development of the pieces gives them real scope and enables them to work efficiently for attack, defense, and maneuvering—gradual improvement of one's position.

There are twenty possible choices for the first move. Which is the best one to play?

ALWAYS START WITH 1 P—K4

Long experience has shown that 1 P—K4 is the best opening move for inexperienced players. One of the virtues of this move is that it helps to control important center squares. This follows from the fact that your opponent cannot afford to place his pieces on squares which are controlled by your Pawns.

This brings us to another vital point. A piece has more scope on a center square or near the center squares than anywhere else on the board. If 1 P—K4 prevents enemy pieces from occupying this desirable sector, this reinforces our confidence in the value of 1 P—K4.

Some of the points discussed thus far are illustrated in Diagram 106. This position arises from the following moves:

WHITE	BLACK
1 P—K4	N—KR3?

This is bad as Black is developing his Knight *away* from the center.

2   P—Q4   ......

Excellent. White secures more control of the center squares, and meanwhile he has opened the diagonals of both Bishops. He has splendid prospects for future development.

2 ......   N—R3?

Worse and worse. He has continued to neglect the center.

Diagram 106
Neglected center

(after 2 ...... N—R3)
White has already achieved a significant advantage. Thanks to his control of the center he will command more of the board and get a more efficient development as the opening unfolds.

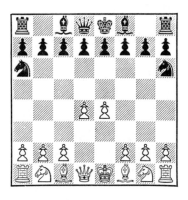

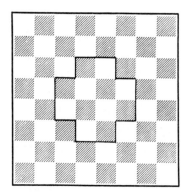

Diagram 107
The vital center

The squares inside the heavily marked border make up the center. Comparing this with Diagram 106, we can see that Black's badly developed Knights have virtually no contact with the center.

To sum up the situation in Diagram 106, we can conclude that even as early as the second move, Black has a strategically lost game!

AVOID SELF-BLOCKING MOVES

There is no surer way to hamper the development process than to make moves with Pawns or pieces that block some indicated future development. Diagrams 108 and 109 are cases in point.

Diagram 108 arises from this sequence: White plays 1 P—K4, and Black replies 1 ...... P—K4. So far, so good. But now White goes astray with 2 N—K2?—a bad move on two counts, as explained in the caption to Diagram 108.

Diagram 108	Diagram 109
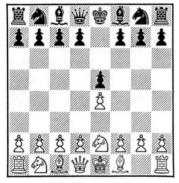	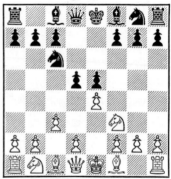

Self-blocking Knight move
(after 2 N—K2)
This move is wrong on two counts. In the first place, it blocks the development of White's King Bishop. Secondly, it gives the Knight an inadequate command of the center. Note that 2 N—KB3! is far superior: it does not block the Bishop, and it gives the Knight a more aggressive bearing on the center.

Self-blocking Pawn move
(after 3 ...... P—Q4!)

White's dubious 3 P—B3 has deprived White of the possibility of playing his Queen Knight to Queen Bishop 3. Black alertly reacts with 3 ...... P—Q4; for if White captures this Pawn, Black replies 4 ...... Q×P and White is unable to menace the Queen with 5 N—B3.

Now consider this sequence:

	WHITE	BLACK
1	P—K4	P—K4
2	N—KB3	N—QB3

The Knight moves on both sides are excellent. Now White fares best with another developing move, say 3 B—N5 or 3 B—B4. Instead there follows:

3	P—B3	P—Q4!

(See Diagram 109)

GUARD YOUR KING

The recommendation to play out your pieces rapidly does not apply to the King, of course. As the whole fate of the game depends on the welfare of this piece, he should be kept as far as possible from the thick of the fight. One of the important reasons for developing your King Knight and King Bishop rapidly is to make room for castling. This tucks the King away at the side of the board and removes him from the center, the scene of intense activity. Many games are lost for failure to follow this all-important rule.

In Diagrams 110 and 111 we see startling retributions follow after careless exposure of the King to decisive attack.

Diagram 110

The harried King

White to move.

WHITE	BLACK
1 Q × KPch!!	......

It is mate next move, for on 1 ...... BP × Q White has 2 B—N5 mate; and on 1 ...... QP × Q there follows 2 B—QB5 mate.

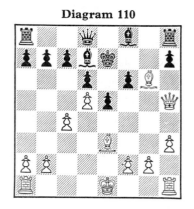

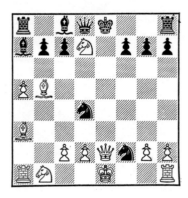

Diagram 111
A fatal double check

Black to move.

WHITE	BLACK
1	N×Q

Black has nothing better, as White's Queen is giving check.

2 N—B6 mate

A brutal double check.

OTHER OPENING POINTERS

The way you play the opening will determine the kind of prospects you will have later on. If you strive for control of the center and further your development and get your King into a safe haven, you will have a promising situation for the middle game.

On the other hand, if you ignore the center, play a whole series of inconclusive Pawn moves, delay the development of your pieces, and leave your King exposed to attack, you are just as surely headed for serious trouble.

Here, then, are a few more simple rules for playing the opening properly. They are easy to apply, yet they can prove immensely valuable.

Inexperienced players are prone to waste time in the opening to snatch insignificant Pawns. The time lost may outweigh by far the value of the Pawn in question. It is therefore a good idea to resist temptation firmly and continue the steady development of your pieces.

Two related faults are attacking prematurely and developing the Queen too soon. This is tempting because of the Queen's enormous powers. But there is also a drawback, precisely because the Queen is so valuable. She can be harried by hostile units of lesser value and must then beat a hasty retreat.

Similarly, premature attacks—usually with the Queen in the forefront—are likely to recoil on the attacker, resulting in considerable loss of time, and sometimes of material as well. Every player has had the experience of succeeding with an unsound attack against weak opposition; but this is clearly something that cannot be recommended in a book!

Finally, avoid the creation of weak points in your position. The most common sin in this respect is optimistically advancing your Pawns beyond the fourth rank in order to drive away enemy pieces. Such advances must be weighed very carefully. Remember that a Pawn once advanced cannot retreat; balance the present good against the potential weakness.

SOME RECOMMENDED OPENINGS

There are many openings with innumerable variations that branch off into thousands of possibilities. The inexperienced player who tries to memorize a few of them finds that he cannot remember them, or that he fails to apply them correctly, or that his opponent avoids playing "by the book."

Fortunately, there is no need for you to make such frustrating attempts to learn the openings. A small repertoire of standard openings will spare you many pitfalls. Here are two standard openings that will help to solve difficulties in this department.

The first of these is the *Giuoco Piano*—this is Italian for "the quiet game." It proceeds in a placid fashion that makes it easy for you to develop your pieces with a minimum of difficulty.

WHITE	BLACK
1 P—K4	P—K4

This advance of the King Pawns, you will recall, has been strongly recommended.

2 N—KB3	. . . . . .

The best development of this Knight—strong action in the

center, coupled with gain of time by attacking Black's King Pawn.

2 ......   N—QB3

Another excellent developing move which guards Black's King Pawn.

3 B—B4   B—B4

Each of these Bishops is on an effective diagonal, bearing down on the King Bishop Pawn. This Pawn is often vulnerable before castling has taken place.

4 P—Q3   ......

This opens the diagonal for White's Queen Bishop.

4 ......   N—B3

The recommended development for this Knight.

5 B—K3   ......

The idea is that if Black plays ...... B×B, White has an open King Bishop file after the recapture P×B.

5 ......   B—N3

A strategic retreat: if White plays B×B, Black replies ...... RP×B with an open Queen Rook file.

6 N—B3   ......

White consistently continues his development.

6 ......   P—Q3

Black opens his Queen Bishop's diagonal.

7 Q—Q2   ......

White reserves the possibility of castling on either wing.

7 ......   B—K3
8 B—N3   ......

These Bishop moves have the same ideas behind them as White's and Black's fifth moves. We now have the situation of Diagram 112.

Diagram 112
Giuoco Piano

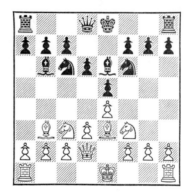

Black to move. The position is even. Both players have pursued their development efficiently without wasting any time. At this point Black will castle and White will follow his example.

Another useful opening for adoption by inexperienced players is the *Scotch Opening*, which starts with these moves:

WHITE	BLACK
1 P—K4	P—K4
2 N—KB3	N—QB3
3 P—Q4	......

This takes up the fight for control of the center. It also opens up the position for White's pieces. For example, White's Queen Bishop is now ready to come into the game.

| 3 ...... | P×P |
| 4 N×P | B—B4 |

A perfectly acceptable alternative is 4 ...... N—B3 (attacking White's King Pawn), which White can answer with 5 N—B3 with even chances.

Diagram 113

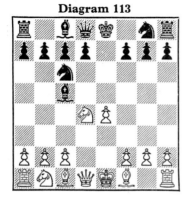

Scotch Opening

White to move. Black threatens to win a piece by capturing White's Knight on the Queen 4 square. White defends most efficiently by developing another piece: 5 B—K3. Generally speaking, the Scotch Opening leads to a little livelier game.

Giuoco Piano and Scotch Openings ■ 73

By following the maxims given here and by adopting the Giuoco Piano and Scotch Opening, inexperienced players will find that they can readily hold their own with players of their own class. In Lessons 6 through 9, we will study a few more openings in depth, and in Lesson 14 you will find a quick survey of other popular openings and defenses.

Basic Checkmates

The basic checkmates are just that: *basic*. These are the fundamental methods of winning a game with a large material advantage. It sounds easy and it is easy; but to the surprisingly large number of players who are not familiar with these methods, winning a won game can be a very arduous and sometimes impossible task.

CHECKMATE WITH THE QUEEN

This is the easiest checkmate—naturally enough, in view of the Queen's enormous powers. The checkmating procedure is illustrated in Diagrams 114 and 115.

Diagram 114
King and Queen vs. *King*

White to move.

	WHITE	BLACK
1	K—B2	K—Q4
2	K—Q3	K—B4
3	Q—B6!	K—Q4
4	Q—K7!	K—B3
5	K—B4	K—N3
6	Q—Q7!	K—R3
7	K—B5	K—R4
8	Q—QR7 mate	

See Diagram 115 for the final position.

The outstandingly important move in this procedure is a long-range Queen move that enormously cuts down the hostile King's mobility. (In this case the move was 3 Q—B6!) Meanwhile the White King approaches as well, and the harmonious co-operation of King and Queen forces the lone King to a side row, where check can then be administered.

Diagram 115
Checkmate by the Queen

CHECKMATE WITH THE ROOK

This mate takes a little longer than the Queen checkmate because the Rook lacks diagonal powers. However, the process is still rather easy. See Diagrams 116 and 117.

Diagram 116
King and Rook vs. King

White to move.

	WHITE	BLACK
1	K—N2	K—Q5
2	K—B2	K—K5
3	K—B3	K—K4
4	K—B4	K—K5
5	R—K1ch!	K—B4
6	K—Q4	K—B5
7	R—KB1ch!	K—N4
8	K—K4	K—N3
9	K—K5	K—N4
10	R—KN1ch!	K—R4
11	K—B4	K—R3

Final Position

12	K—B5	K—R2
13	K—B6	K—R1
14	K—B7	K—R2
15	R—R1 mate	

Basic Checkmates ■ 75

Diagram 117

Checkmate by the Rook

Note the position of the Kings, directly facing each other, with the Black King trapped on a side row. The technique of forcing the Black King back to the last row is very instructive. The key move here is 5 R—K1ch!, played at a point where the two Kings face each other, so that the Black King is forced to give way. (The process is repeated at

White's seventh and tenth move.) Master this principle and you will find that the Rook checkmate is child's play.

CHECKMATE WITH THE TWO BISHOPS

A single Bishop, as we know, cannot give checkmate; but two Bishops can do so. The process should take about 17 moves at most from the least favorable position—one in which the lone King is in the center of the board, and the stronger side's King is far away. To shorten the process somewhat, we start the mating process from a more favorable position. In any event, the underlying idea remains the same: the lone King must be forced to a corner square. See Diagrams 118 and 119.

Diagram 118

King and two Bishops vs. King

White to move.

	WHITE	BLACK
1	B—Q1	K—B5
2	B—QB2	K—N5
3	K—Q5	K—N4
4	B—QB5!	K—R3
5	K—B6	K—R4
6	B—Q6	K—R3
7	B—N4	K—R2
8	K—B7	K—R3

	WHITE	BLACK
9	B—Q3ch	K—R2
10	B—QB5ch	K—R1
11	B—K4 mate	

Diagram 119

Checkmate by the two Bishops

As you have noticed, this process requires the closest kind of co-operation between the Bishops and their King. The significant moves here are 3 K—Q5! and 4 B—QB5! Each of these moves plays an essential role in cutting down the mobility of the lone King. Only by eliminating the lone King's access to certain squares can he be forced to the side and then to a corner square.

Basic Checkmates ■ 77

CHECKMATE WITH BISHOP AND KNIGHT

This mate requires more moves than the mate with the two Bishops. But it is highly rewarding because it calls for first-class co-operation on the part of the checkmating pieces. The checkmate can only be effected by driving the lone King to a corner square. In addition, this corner square must be of the same color as the one that the Bishop travels on. If your Bishop moves on white squares, for example, the lone King will be checkmated on a white corner square.

The checkmate process is illustrated in Diagrams 120 to 122. The ending is presented here in a somewhat advanced stage, after the lone King has been driven to a side row. You are now familiar with the technique for accomplishing this—systematically cutting down the lone King's access to squares and gradually forcing him back.

Diagram 120
King and Bishop and Knight vs.
King

White to move.

	WHITE	BLACK
1	K—B6	K—R1
2	N—B7ch	K—N1
3	B—B5	K—B1
4	B—R7!	K—K1
5	N—K5!	K—B1
6	N—Q7ch	K—K1
7	K—K6	K—Q1
8	K—Q6	K—K1
9	B—N6ch!	K—Q1
10	B—R5	K—B1

See Diagram 121

White has made considerable progress toward the white corner square.

11	N—B5!	K—Q1
12	N—N7ch	K—B1
13	K—B6	K—N1
14	K—N6	K—B1
15	B—N4ch	K—N1
16	B—B5	K—R1

Now the end is very near.

17	N—B5	K—N1
18	N—R6ch	K—R1
19	B—K4 mate	

See Diagram 122

Diagram 121

Checkmate by Bishop and Knight

This is the basic checkmate which calls for the most sustained effort and the most harmonious co-operation of all three checkmating pieces. It is an excellent ending to practice because it gives such a good idea of how the pieces work together.

Diagram 122

The Endgame

The endgame, as its name indicates, is the final stage of the game. It is highly simplified, with most of the pieces gone; the Queens are rarely left on the board. Precisely because the position is so simplified, this is the stage in which a player has the best chance of turning a material advantage to account; the prospective loser has comparatively little chance to affect the issue by trying to introduce complications.

It is one of the great weaknesses of average players that they underestimate the importance of the endgame. Ability to play this phase of the game well can become one of your most valuable assets. By studying the standard endings in this lesson you can create many favorable opportunities for winning.

The endings will be dealt with in greater detail in Lessons 10 through 13.

The average player can enormously increase his endgame skill and the number of his victories if he comes to realize that the most important phase of endgame play revolves about the promotion of a Pawn. For the successful queening of a Pawn gives him a whole Queen ahead, enabling him to deliver checkmate (Diagrams 114 and 115) without the slightest trouble. It is at this point that we can appreciate the fact that the "lowly" Pawn is a pearl of great price.

Diagram 123
Basic King and Pawn ending
White to move.

WHITE	BLACK
1 P—Q6	K—Q1
2 P—Q7	K—K2
3 K—B7 and wins	

White continues 4 P—Q8/Q and forces checkmate, as in Diagram 114.

Diagram 124

The power of passed Pawns

White to move. White has two
passed Pawns—there are no
hostile Pawns to stop their
advance. In fact, White wins
without his King's help.

	WHITE	BLACK
1	P—N6	K—B3
2	P—B6	K—K3
3	P—N7	K—B2
4	P—B7 and wins	

Diagram 125

The distant passed Pawn

White to move. His Rook
Pawn, the distant passed
Pawn, cannot be stopped.

	WHITE	BLACK
1	P—R4	K—B1
2	P—R5	K—K1
3	P—R6	K—Q1
4	P—R7 and wins	

*Black's King was too far
away from the critical sector.*

Diagram 126

White to move.

	WHITE	BLACK
1	P—R5!	K—B3
2	K—K5!	K—N4
3	K—B6	K×P
4	K×NP	K—N3
5	K×P	K—B3
6	K—K6	K—B2
7	K—K7!	K—B1
8	P—B5 and wins	

Black's King was drawn off.

*The power of the distant passed
Pawn*

Diagram 127

White must preserve his Pawn!

White to move.

WHITE	BLACK
1 B—B4!	P—Q4

If 1 . . . K—B2; 2 P—B5! wins.

| 2 P—B5! | . . . . . . |

Here 2 P×P?? draws.

2	K—R3
3 K—Q4	K—N4
4 B—K3!	K—KN3
5 K—K5!	K—B5
6 K—Q6	K—N4
7 B—B2	K—R3
8 K×BP and wins	

White will queen his Pawn.

Diagram 128

A neat trick

White to move.

WHITE	BLACK
1 R—KR8!	R×P

Otherwise White queens his Pawn.

| 2 R—R7ch and wins | |

Black's Rook is lost. This stratagem turns up fairly frequently in Rook and Pawn endings. It is sometimes called the "X-ray" attack.

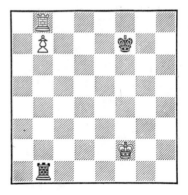

Diagram 129
A standard Rook and Pawn ending

White to move.

	WHITE	BLACK
1	R—Q1ch!	K—B2
2	R—Q4!	R—N8
3	K—K7	R—K8ch
4	K—B6	R—KB8ch
5	K—K6	R—K8ch
6	K—B5	R—KB8ch
7	R—KB4 and wins	

The Pawn must queen. 1 R—Q1ch! drives Black's King away.

How to Salvage Lost Endgames

Quite naturally we all concentrate on winning. But it is also important to be able to snatch a draw from a lost game. Indeed, our relief and gratification at such a last-minute rescue make up one of the most enjoyable aspects of chess.

As it happens, there are quite a few valuable standard positions in which it is possible to stave off defeat—in some cases, with a Queen down! Here are some of the more common ones (Diagrams 130 to 137).

White to move.

	WHITE	BLACK
1	P—Q7ch	K—Q1
2	K—Q6	Drawn

Black is stalemated. White had no choice at move 2, as he needed to keep his Pawn protected. With Black to move in the diagram position, White wins. See Diagram 123.

Diagram 130
Only a draw

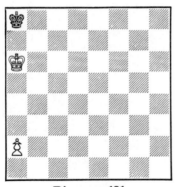

Diagram 131
White cannot win

White to move.

	WHITE	BLACK
1	K—N6	K—N1
2	P—R4	K—R1
3	P—R5	K—N1
4	P—R6	K—R1
5	P—R7	Drawn

Black is stalemated. The Rook Pawn can never win if the hostile King is at or near his Rook 1.

There are some cases in which a Rook Pawn does not win even when supported by a Bishop. In Diagram 132 White wins because his Bishop commands the queening square. In Diagram 133 White cannot win because his Bishop does not command the queening square.

Diagram 132
White wins

White to move.

	WHITE	BLACK
1	B—Q5ch	K—N1
2	P—R7ch	K—B1
3	P—R8/Qch and wins	

White will checkmate very shortly. In Diagram 133, however, White's Bishop is on the wrong color.

Diagram 133

White draws

White to move.

	WHITE	BLACK
1	K—R5	K—R2
2	K—N5	K—R1
3	K—N6	K—N1
4	B—K5ch	K—R1!

Drawn. Any effort to win will only stalemate Black; for example, 5 P—R7.

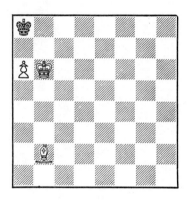

The advantage of an extra Pawn in Bishop and Pawn endings and Rook and Pawn endings is generally decisive. Yet there are exceptions, and two of these are shown in Diagrams 134 and 135.

Diagram 134

Bishops on opposite colors

It does not matter who moves first here. When one Bishop moves on white squares and the other on black, the win often becomes impossible even where a player is two Pawns to the good. This applies particularly to the above position, where the Pawns ought to be on black *squares. As matters stand, White can never play P—B6ch because Bishop's Black is an efficient blockader. If White had a Bishop on black squares he would win rather easily.*

Diagram 135
White cannot win

Black to move.

	WHITE	BLACK
1	......	K—N2
2	K—N5	R—QB3
3	P—B5	R—QN3
4	R—QR2	R—Q3
5	R—R7ch	K—N1
6	P—B6	R—Q8!
7	K—N6	R—KN8ch
8	K—B5	K—B1
9	K—K6	R—K8ch
10	K—B5	K—N1

Drawn. White can make no headway.

It verges on the incredible that a player can draw with only a Pawn against a Queen. Yet there are certain typical situations in which this happens. They are shown in Diagrams 136 and 137.

Diagram 136
Black draws

White to move. To stop the Pawn from queening, he must check.

	WHITE	BLACK
1	Q—KN3ch	K—R8

White cannot win. If he makes a Queen move to relieve the stalemate position, Black moves his King, again threatening to queen.

Black to move. The right drawing method is to play the King into the corner.

WHITE	BLACK
1	K—R8!

Now Black threatens to queen the Pawn. If White replies 2 Q×P, Black is stalemated. No check will accomplish anything.

Diagram 137
Black draws

From your study of these remarkable positions, you have learned how it is possible on occasion to extract a creditable and satisfying draw from what seems a hopelessly lost game. The knowledge thus gained should be of use to you time and again in your own games.

Here are two quick mates you should be aware of.

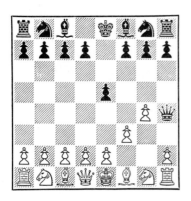

Diagram 138

	WHITE	BLACK
1	P—KB3?	P—K4
2	P—KN4??	Q—R5 mate

"FOOL'S MATE"

White's foolish, weakening Pawn moves opened the gates to the enemy. This is the quickest checkmate you can bring off in a game.

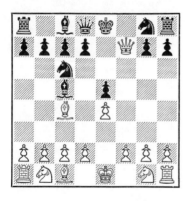

Diagram 139

	WHITE	BLACK
1	P—K4	P—K4
2	B—B4	B—B4
3	Q—R5	......

Black is checkmated

"SCHOLAR'S MATE"

White threatens Q×KPch, but what is much more important, he also threatens Q×BP mate.

Black sees the first threat, but overlooks the second threat.

3	......	N—QB3??

The right way was 3 ...... Q—K2, guarding his King Pawn *and* at the same time preventing the threatened mate.

4	Q×BP mate	

This mate is a good example of the suddenness with which a gross oversight in the opening can lead to a quick decision.

"Scholar's Mate" has caught unwary victims for centuries.

Diagram 140

LESSON 5:
SOME INSTRUCTIVE GAMES

There are several good reasons for studying these games carefully. One is that if you have never played a game these brief encounters will give you the feel of an actual game. Another valuable aspect of the games is that they illustrate common faults and show you how drastically these faults can be punished. Finally, these examples teach an important lesson in showing how quickly a game of chess can be won—or lost.

CENTER GAME

	WHITE	BLACK
1	P—K4	P—K4
2	P—Q4	. . . . . .

Theoretically this advance in the center is commendable, but it has the drawback of leading to a loss of time. The previously recommended 2 N—KB3 is better.

2	. . . . . .	P×P
3	Q×P	. . . . . .

White's Queen comes into play prematurely and is at once exposed to attack.

3	. . . . . .	N—QB3!

This is the move that spoils the opening for White.

White to move. Black's Queen Knight attacks the White Queen, forcing White to lose a move in bringing the Queen to a safe post.

Diagram 141

Position after Black's third move

4 Q—K3   N—B3

Already Black is distinctly ahead in development.

5 B—B4   N—K4

Generally speaking, you are better off not to move the same
piece more than once in the opening. However, since the move
is bound up with a threat (......N×B), the principle can be
waived here.

(See Diagram 142)

White to move. Though Black has violated opening theory
by moving his Knight twice, he is gaining time by attacking
White's Bishop. Also, he is laying the groundwork for a very
subtle trap.

6 B—N3   B—N5ch

A very tricky move. White would be well advised to counter

Diagram 142
Position after Black's fifth move

this check with a developing move, say 7 N—QB3 or perhaps 7 B—Q2.

7   P—QB3   . . . . . .

This interposition is not fatal, but it is certainly questionable. Note that White's Queen Bishop Pawn no longer controls White's Queen 3 square. This is a very important factor in the coming play.

7 . . . . . .   B—B4!

(See Diagram 143)

White to move. If White captures the unprotected Bishop with his Queen, Black replies . . . . . . N—Q6ch forking the White King and Queen.

In the face of Black's insidious Knight fork menace, White must beat a prudent retreat with his Queen. The question is,

Diagram 143

Position after Black's seventh move

where? For example, 8 Q—B4?? would not do because of 8
...... N—Q6ch still winning by means of the Knight fork.

8 Q—N3??   ......

A mistake, although it must be admitted that Black's startling
refutation was not easy to foresee.

White's best was 8 Q—K2, although it would have meant
that White had taken *three* moves to get to a square that could
have been reached in *one* move with proper play.

8 ......   B×Pch!!
Resigns

White to move. White must capture the Bishop because
there is a double attack on his King and Queen. If White
captures the Bishop with his Queen, Black replies 9 ......
N—Q6ch. If White captures the Bishop with his King, Black

Diagram 144

Why does White resign?

replies 9 ...... N×Pch. In either case, Black wins the White Queen with a Knight forking check and further resistance is hopeless. So White prefers to resign.

BEWARE OF THOUGHTLESS DEVELOPMENT

We have just seen an example of indiscriminate development. This is a fault which almost automatically brings its own punishment. Here is another example of the same theme:

ALEKHINE'S DEFENSE

WHITE	BLACK
1 P—K4	N—KB3

This unconventional Knight development has the virtue of

developing the Knight toward the center. Yet its consequences can be very tricky. It is therefore best left to highly experienced players.

Diagram 145
Black's Knight move is provocative

White to move. He decides to drive off the Knight, at the possible risk of weakening his Pawns by unduly optimistic advances.

2	P—K5	N—Q4
3	P—QB4	......

Black to move. Black's Knight is driven away from the center. On the other hand, White's Pawn moves are cone tributing nothing to his development. So far, the disadvantages cancel each other.

Diagram 146

Position after White's third move

| 3 | ...... | N—N3 |
| 4 | P—Q4 | ...... |

Still another Pawn move, but this one has the virtue of opening the White Queen Bishop's diagonal and supporting his advanced King Pawn.

Black's indicated reply is 4 ...... P—Q3, putting some restraint on the White Pawns and opening up the diagonal of his Queen Bishop. Instead, he commits a frightful blunder.

| 4 | ...... | N—B3?? |

Unbelievable as it may seem, Black is now forced to lose a piece, no matter how he plays.

| 5 | P—Q5! | ...... |

This surprise move wins a piece against any play by Black.

Alekhine's Defense ■ 95

Diagram 147

Position after White's fifth move.
Black is left without a good reply.

Black to move. The apparently safe 5 ...... N—N1 will not do because of 6 P—B5 and the unfortunate Knight has no retreat. On the other hand, if Black tries 5 ...... N—N5 White still wins a piece with 6 P—B5! forcing 6 ...... N/N3 × P, whereupon 7 P—QR3 compels Black to lose one of the Knights.

	5	N × KP

On the face of it, this is an easy way out. But Black is lost just the same.

	6 P—B5	N/N3—B5

Black's Knights are vulnerable.

	7 P—B4!	......

Diagram 148
One of Black's Knights is lost

Black to move. If his attacked Knight retreats, White can simply reply 8 B × N with a piece to the good. Black resigned a few moves later. The rest of the game does not concern us.

WATCH FOR HOSTILE THREATS

There is no surer way to lose than by ignoring your opponent's threats. That is why you must ask yourself after every move by your opponent, "What's he up to? What does he threaten? Can he capture any of my forces?" The following brief game shows what can happen when this self-questioning process is ignored.

FRENCH DEFENSE

WHITE	BLACK
1 P—K4	P—K3

A change from the openings we have seen so far. Instead of replying ...... P—K4, Black prefers to prepare to dispute the center by 2 ...... P—Q4. This is an acceptable method, if Black bears in mind that his Queen Bishop may be somewhat lacking in mobility.

2 P—Q4	P—Q4
3 P—K5	......

Diagram 149
White strives for "encirclement"

Black to move. The presence of White's King Pawn on King 5 has a very cramping effect on Black's development.

For example, he is unable to play . . . . . . N—KB3—the best development for his King Knight.

      3 . . . . . .   P—QB4!

Excellent. By trying to remove White's Queen Pawn (which supports White's King Pawn), Black has taken the first step towards freedom.

      4 Q—N4?!   . . . . . .

Another move about which we have mixed feelings. One must always be suspicious about an early development of the Queen, as she is often exposed to attack in such situations (see Diagram 141). On the other hand, the Queen move is consistent with White's master plan—cramping Black's game. In this case, Black is unable to develop his King Bishop—at least for the time being.

      4 . . . . . .   P×P

Black carries out his strategic plan consistently—first he removes White's Queen Pawn, so that he can concentrate on his King Pawn. Also he hopes for 5 Q×QP, which he will answer with 5 . . . . . . N—QB3! gaining valuable time.

      5 N—KB3   . . . . . .

White refuses to lose time with repeated Queen moves.

      5 . . . . . .   P—B4

Black attacks the White Queen, but at the cost of weakening his King's position and depriving himself of the opportunity of ridding himself subsequently of the burdensome hostile King Pawn with . . . . . . P—B3.

Black had a better course in 5 . . . . . . N—QB3 followed by . . . . . . KN—K2 and then . . . . . . N—N3. In this way Black would have been well on the way to carrying out his development in an orderly fashion and at the same time he would have a strong counter-attack on White's King Pawn.

      6 Q—N3   N—QB3
      7 B—K2   . . . . . .

Diagram 150
Black must be alert

Black to move. White's quiet development of his King Bishop is bound up with a subtle trap that Black completely misses. Had he realized his opponent's devilish design he would have played 7 ...... Q—N3 or 7 ...... Q—B2.

       7 ......   B—Q2?

Black innocently misses the point, playing just the very move that makes White's trap work.

       8 N×P!!   ......

Black to move. Here is what White hopes for:

	WHITE	BLACK
8	......	N×N??
9	B—R5ch	P—KN3
10	Q×Pch!!	P×Q
11	B×Pch	K—K2

Diagram 151

Position after White's eighth move

What does White have in mind?

12	B—N5ch	N—B3
13	B×N mate!	

But this is only an imaginary continuation, so let us go back to the position of Diagram 151 and see what happens in the actual game.

8	......	N×N??

He captures the Knight after all. By declining the Knight and playing some reasonable move such as 8 ...... Q—N3, he would still have had a game of sorts.

9	B—R5ch	......

So far the game has proceeded as in our hypothetical continuation. But now Black varies, as he realizes that 9 ...... P—KN3 must lose.

9 ...... K—K2

Black reckons smugly on 10 B—N5ch, N—KB3; 11 P × Nch, P × P when he threatens ...... P × B as well as ...... N × Pch winning White's Queen Rook. But he gets a rude jolt.

10 Q—QR3 mate!

Diagram 152
An airplane check

Black has been checkmated by a remarkable Queen move. This completes the punishment inflicted on him for his failure to see through White's plans.

The following lessons will give you a deeper insight into the game and will further your progress.

LESSON 6: HOW TO THINK
AS A CHESS PLAYER

Many chess players tell me that they are deeply troubled by their failure to improve. Game after game, year after year, they repeat their same old mistakes.

While it is true that "learning by doing" is an important element in acquiring a skill, little improvement is possible when you do not know the reasoning behind the doing. If you are such a player I would say, "Don't waste your time playing! Read books instead."

This advice may seem strange, but it has logic behind it. If you've been playing chess—or any game—for years without improving, you are obviously using a wrong approach. You may doggedly resolve to do better, to be more careful, to avoid oversights and blunders—all in vain.

The Need for Guidance

Your studying must have direction. It must be based not only on your experience, but also on the experiences of the millions of other people who have played chess.

Then too, your study must have guidance. You may make the same mistake thousands of times over without realizing that it is a mistake. You may be relying, in vain, on certain opening lines of play that are definitely faulty and that leave you at a disadvantage from the very start. For any one of several reasons, you may not make the most of your middle-game chances. You may be so prejudiced against playing endgames that you do not handle them well.

The idea behind this and the next three lessons is to supply the kind of guidance you need, in the form of *complete games*. Studying isolated positions can be instructive, but best of all are games from actual tournament play. You have a chance to study each game from the first groping stage to the formation of large-scale plans, the maneuvering for position in the middle game, the evolution of a decisive attack, and the crisp, brilliant execution that winds up each game with a satisfactory close.

The ideal situation is to set up the diagrams on your board and actually play out and study each move before going on to the next.

Psychological Factors

But there is much more to it than that. In your own games success alternates with failure, contentment with dissatisfaction, hope with despair, elation with disgust; each game is full of ups and downs. These alternations of mood help to make chess exciting, but they also have another effect. The way you feel at any stage of the game will profoundly affect the strength or weakness of your play. A player who fights back hard in a difficult position is obviously going to get more out of it than a player who is full of black despair. These psychological factors are particularly emphasized in Lessons 7, 8 and 9.

The Method of Study

What is the method I use in these lessons, and why do I use it? Just as most players are satisfied with rough-and-ready practical play without looking into the underlying theory, many writers are satisfied to expound theory without considering the thorny practical problems of actual play. I have tried to combine the best of both approaches.

The best way is to study games from start to finish. This enables you to see the individual details that go into an actual game; it also enables you to see the game as a whole, or at least as a composite of several broadly defined stages.

Soon you observe that certain elements stand out. At the beginning of the game, as you've seen in earlier lessons, there is a crying need for development—rapid deployment of your pieces—and for safeguarding the King. Later in this lesson, you will see how neglected development can prove disastrous.

Neglected Development

There is something very instructive in the way that neglected development is punished in this game. You may expect to see the punishment administered quickly and flamboyantly, with a shower of sacrifices and a quick checkmate. In "real life" this is not too likely, unless the neglect of development is really crass. In this first game, for example, Black's bad judgment in move 4 on page 116 is the move that leads inexorably but unsensationally to his downfall.

In fact, this move is so unobtrusive that many a reader, studying the game without notes, might be quite bewildered if called upon to point out where Black went wrong. If the student does not realize that 4 ...... N×KP? is a serious mistake, then he misses the whole point of the game. On the other hand, once the nature of this mistake is pointed out to him, he can see what consequences it produces. In that case, the game becomes clear, logical, understandable. The lesson is clearly brought home to him that 4 ...... N×KP? is a mistake that results in steadily accumulating difficulties.

Thus the chain of cause and effect is clearly established. A complete game without notes is worthless to the student; a precept without an example from actual play is not much better. Only the combination I use here—the practical game plus the theoretical explanation—can really help you as a chess student.

Given this type of material, you learn two things. First, you are made to realize that if you neglect development, you are likely to be punished drastically for it. Secondly, if your opponent is the culprit who neglects development, you learn how to exploit such lapses. This is true progress.

Play Vigorously

In Lesson 7 we will advance to more difficult problems. The grand underlying theme of this game might be stated in one word: "determination." Most of us would rather attack than defend, but you cannot always have your choice. Whichever task fate assigns you, you must play with determination. An attack that is managed half-heartedly will never succeed. A defense that is conducted lackadaisically, is sure to collapse.

Of course, no one can change character overnight. But observation of other players' difficulties can tell you a great deal about your own failings. It can give you an insight into the kind of qualities you need to develop, as well as the kind that you need to curb.

Broad Strategy

Theoretical maxims and enthusiastic exhortations will not get you far. The games you will study here actually are grim struggles between two players of flesh and blood. I explain them in terms of broad plans, and at the same time fit in the move-by-move progress of the play. You see how the moves fit into the plans, and how the plans themselves gradually evolve and change. This is an important aspect of realistic study.

A great general once defined strategy as "the development of an original idea in accordance with changing circumstances." Those last two words are like the small print in a contract: they are enormously important but few people pay attention to them.

Most chess players conduct their games without a plan. But when they finally do start planning, they are much too stubborn and intractable. They do not realize that changing circumstances require changes and modifications in the original plan. In fact, if the player is too inflexible, his plan—to mix a metaphor—may wind up as a millstone around his neck.

The Fighter Wins

In this respect, Lesson 7 is enormously instructive. White (the attacker) is a wonderful fighter. He flourishes on tactical difficulties and no problem terrifies him; at the same time he is remarkably elastic, accommodating himself to every new situation. He is inflexible on only one point: he means to win, regardless of the situation. He is a fighter who does not know when to let go.

This can be a dangerous trait in a chess player. In the game in Lesson 7 this quality does the winner no harm, because he is a much better player than his opponent, and he can therefore afford to take risks. In effect, White is giving his opponent odds—the odds of risking the loss of the game.

As for Black, what kind of player is he? Timid, irresolute, appalled by White's grandiose bluffing. He survives every crisis by dogged plugging, only to succumb to the last, comparatively minor crisis, when he is completely worn out by the troubles he has had to endure.

Building an Attack

In Lesson 8 you have the opportunity of watching the build-up of a powerful attack. This provides a much-needed lesson to those who imagine that an attack is a matter of inspired genius, or that it "suddenly" appears where it did not exist before. Actually, a powerful attack comes about by careful preparation, abetted by the opponent's shortcomings. How these factors mesh together is convincingly demonstrated in this game. You should read the introductory comment to Lesson 8 with great care. It shows that the origin of every attack lies in some prior mistake by your opponent. Once he has made himself vulnerable, your attack can take the center of the stage. But because attacking play is showy, brilliant, often breathtakingly lively, you may be so entranced that you forget the prosaic beginnings that led up to the attack.

By thus gaining an insight into the mechanics and preparation of attack, you acquire an understanding of chess that will improve your playing strength enormously. To know how to prepare an attack is planning in the best sense.

Positional Gambits

The game in Lesson 9 is the most difficult of all, and also the one which offers the most valuable instruction. A strong chess player uses and defends against gambits regularly. A gambit is a move or series of moves in which a player gives up a Pawn or a piece or several pieces voluntarily to gain an advantageous position. The art of playing positional gambits is one of the most important talents a chess player can master. It requires a keen understanding of the speculative attack, and of your opponent. Nevertheless, the student who has read the earlier lessons attentively should find this lesson particularly useful.

And what do we mean by reading "attentively"? Any skill that is worth acquiring calls for a good deal of drudgery. No matter whether you are learning to swim, to write shorthand, or to drive a car, you are reconciled to the fact that you will need a good deal of practice and a good deal of repetition. Nobody begrudges spending hours and hours of practice on golf, and paying comparatively large sums for lessons.

Yet when it comes to chess, with its infinity of subtle detail, some people expect to become masters without concentrated study for at least two weeks. When they realize that chess requires real application, they become disenchanted.

Play and Replay

I have written these 14 lessons on the assumption (or in the expectation) that after you have finished these lessons you will want to improve still further and be willing to read, to reflect, to go deeply into study. I hope that you will not be satisfied with one reading.

As in other fields, you will benefit enormously by playing and replaying the games in this book again and again. Every time you play over these games, you will see more in them, learn more, appreciate them better, become a better player and improve the chess you produce in your own games.

Again, with repeated playing over of these games, you will begin to *foresee* consequences; you will observe sooner the unfolding of plans; you will relish the keen struggle of threat and counterthreat; you will develop your own preferences and your own style.

Repeatedly you will see *types* that you will want to use in your own games; you will understand mistakes and how to avoid them; you will learn how to make and develop plans; you will become adept at modifying plans as changing circumstances dictate.

How to Study Chess

Finally, a word on how to study the following games. *Do not omit playing over the variations in the notes.* Many readers find such variations inconvenient or confusing, and therefore avoid them. Yet these variations can sometimes tell you more than the "text" moves that were actually played! In any event, your study of a game is vastly incomplete without an examination of these alternative lines of play.

The sensible way to tackle them is to play over the actual moves on a big board, and play the variations in the notes with a smaller or pocket set. In that way you will get the utmost out of the variations without running any risk of losing a position on the big board.

So, to get the most out of these lessons, do not be afraid to play over these games repeatedly. Your understanding of the play will increase each time; your pleasure in the games will be heightened. Above all, you will play better chess in your own games.

HOW TO ATTACK
AN UNDEVELOPED POSITION

Every chess player frequently has to solve the problem of how to proceed in a situation where he has more pieces in play than his opponent. If he attacks too soon, he may dissipate his whole advantage; he may even call forth a powerful counter-attack from his opponent.

On the other hand, holding back the attack unduly may have an unsatisfactory result too. It gives the opponent time to get more pieces into the game, to consolidate his position, to make his pieces co-operate.

What do we mean by attacking too soon, or too late? How do we determine the timing? To a considerable degree, timing depends on development: how many units do you have in play, and how many does your opponent have in play?

Vitally important, too, is how these developed pieces are functioning. Are they active, or do they play a minor role in the game? Can they attack? threaten? capture? give check? sacrifice themselves for a greater goal?

In the course of every attack, there comes a point of highest efficiency—when your pieces are developed in the most aggressive way, and when resistance to their inroads is still puny. That is the time to strike, and the time that offers the greatest chances of success.

The following game shows how a player starts out to get an

advantage in development; and how, once he has achieved that advantage, he goes on to organize a winning attack based on his noticeable lead in development and the more aggressive placement of his pieces.

TWO KNIGHTS' DEFENSE

WHITE	BLACK
1 P—K4	P—K4

This advance of the King Pawn is always an excellent choice for the first move. It opens lines of development for the pieces and starts the struggle for control of the center squares, the most important sector of the board.

Experience has shown repeatedly that the greater control a player has of the center squares, the more mobility his pieces will have. You will see this proposition illustrated again and again throughout this book.

Even at this early stage you can see some of the benefits involved from controlling center squares.

Consider the position of White's King Pawn. It controls White's Queen 5 square, for example. That means that no Black piece can occupy the square in question. (If a Black piece did move there, White's King Pawn could capture it.)

In playing 1 ...... P—K4 in reply, Black was following the same train of thought to secure his fair share of the center.

2 N—KB3

Diagram 153

(Position after 2 N—KB3)
White has developed his King Knight to its best square.

How to Attack ■ 111

The emphasis is now on bringing out ("developing") one's pieces. The faster this is done, the better.

But fast development, all by itself, is not necessarily a virtue.

Playing 2 N—KR3? or 2 N—K2? would also be fast development—but it would not be good.

At King Rook 3 the Knight would be far from the center and would take little part in the game.

At King 2 the Knight would not be developed with maximum effect. Worst yet, here *the Knight would block the development of White's King Bishop*.

At King Bishop 3, however, the King Knight is most efficient. It bears down on White's Queen 4 square and King 5 square—two center squares of the greatest importance. Thus the Knight is posted to good advantage.

Another excellent feature of 2 N—KB3 is that it attacks Black's King Pawn. Development with a threat is *development with gain of time*.

Black's main job is to defend his King Pawn. He can accomplish this in various ways—by a nondeveloping move, by a poor developing move, or by a good developing move.

Of course, when the choice is presented to you in this fashion, you say, "By all means, let's have a good developing move!"

But the average player, unaware of the fateful choice confronting him, may play a move that has serious drawbacks.

For example: Black can defend his King Pawn with a nondeveloping move, say 2 ...... P—Q3. In this case he has guarded his King Pawn efficiently, but he has neglected his development—he has failed to bring out a piece.

Or Black can guard his King Pawn with an inferior developing move, such as 2 .. ... B—Q3?

In that event Black has developed his King Bishop, to be sure. But he has blocked his Queen Pawn, which is now unable to advance. *This in turn means that he cannot develop his Queen Bishop.*

Thus we find that 2 ..... B—Q3?, though it develops a piece, actually damages Black's prospects of effective development.

The best move is:

2 ..... N—QB3

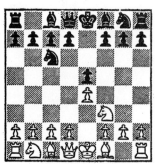

Diagram 154

(Position after 2 ..... N—QB3)

Black has played a good developing move. His Queen Knight guards his King Pawn. At the same time the Knight bears down on important center squares: Black's King 4 and Queen 5 squares.

Now White wants to continue his development. The logical piece to play out is his King Bishop. (Once he moves this piece he is ready to castle his King into safety.)

So White plays:

3 B—B4 ......

Diagram 155

(Position after 3 B—B4)

White's developed Bishop bears down on Black's vulnerable point: his King Bishop 2 square.

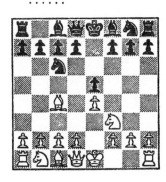

At Queen Bishop 4 White's King Bishop bears down powerfully against Black's King Bishop Pawn. Black must reckon, for example, with an *eventual* N—N5 with double attack against this Pawn. Or, if he is experienced and sophisticated, he may deliberately permit this attack in the hope of getting compensation elsewhere.

Attacking Two Knights' Defense ■ 113

For the average player, however, the threat against Black's King Bishop 2 square is a serious one and should be avoided or neutralized.

Thus Black's safest move is 3 ...... B—B4, preparing to castle and thus to utilize the Black King Rook to lend additional protection to his King Bishop Pawn.

In this game, however, Black deliberately looks for trouble.

3 ...... N—B3

This is a developing move, and it also has the merit of attacking White's King Pawn. However, the move allows the dangerous possible reply 4 N—N5, and is therefore best avoided by inexperienced players.

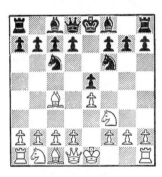

Diagram 156

(Position after 3 ...... N—B3)
By playing his last move, Black deliberately courts complications. White has to make up his mind to accept the challenge, or ignore it.

(Note that *before* 3 ...... N—B3, White could not venture on N—N5, as his advanced Knight would be captured by Black's Queen.)

Now White has to make up his mind whether he wants to play 4 N—N5, with double attack on Black's King Bishop Pawn.

Here is one complicated possibility: 4 N—N5, P—Q4; 5 P×P, N×P!; 6 N×BP?! (the famous Fried Liver Attack), K×N; 7 Q—B3ch, K—K3; 8 N—B3, QN—N5!; 9 Q—K4, P—B3; 10 P—Q4, K—Q2! and Black's King should escape with his life.

Another wild possibility: 4 N—N5, B—B4!? (very daring); 5 N×BP, B×Pch!? (Black is determined to prove that White's King Bishop 2 square is also vulnerable); 6 K×B, N×Pch;

7 K—K3? (too risky), Q—K2; 8 K×N, P—Q4ch; 9 B×P, Q—R5ch!; 10 P—N4, B×P; 11 B×Nch, B—Q2 dis ch!; 12 K—K3, Q—Q5ch; 13 K—K2, P×B! and Black has a winning attack. (His immediate threat is 14 ...... B—N5ch winning the Queen.)

These variations are inordinately complicated, and you may well be appalled by their complexity. But there is no need for you to dwell on them in great detail.

By merely glancing over them cursorily you realize that White does well to select a line of play that is less involved and less risky. The moral is that in your own games it is often wiser to choose a simple, safe course than one which is full of risk and likely to get out of hand.

4   P—Q4   ......

White chooses a sensible alternative. He gains more ground in the center, and at the same time he prepares for the development of his Queen Bishop. Furthermore the move has the additional virtue of confronting Black with a troublesome problem.

Diagram 157

(Position after 4 P—Q4)
White has seized the initiative in the center. Black must choose between 4 ...... P×P or 4 N×KP in order to get a fair share of the center.

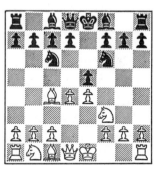

For years the recommended book move for Black has been 4 ...... P×P.

To be sure, 5 P—K5 in reply looks menacing, but Black has a sturdy, serviceable reply in 5 ...... P—Q4! Then, after 6 P×N, P×B or 6 B—QN5, N—K5 Black's situation in the center is even more favorable than White's.

Attacking Two Knights' Defense   ■   115

The other leading possibility after 4 ...... P×P is 5 Castles, N×P; 6 R—K1, P—Q4. Despite his two Pawns minus, White need not be disheartened, as he can play 7 B×P!, Q×B; 8 N—B3! (very pretty), Q—QR4; 9 N×N, B—K3; 10 N/K4—N5, Castles. White regains the sacrificed material, but Black castles his King into safety and gets a comfortable development.

4 ......   N×KP?

But this is inferior. The Knight moves a second time, to a square where he will be exposed to attack and will consequently have to move a third time very soon. Such serious neglect of development is bound to have a bad effect on Black's position.

5 P×P   ......

Diagram 158

(Position after 5 P×P)
Already White has a brutal threat: 6 Q—Q5 threatening 7 Q×BP mate and also 7 Q×N. This induces Black to retreat the menaced Knight.

To meet White's nasty threat of Q—Q5, Black moves his unfortunate Knight from the King 5 square—the third move with this Knight out of five moves!

5 ......   N—B4

6 N—B3   ......

Even at this early stage we can discern the coming possibilities. Not only has Black wasted time with his King Knight; he has also deprived his King Bishop of his best square, Queen Bishop 4. Hence the Bishop must make do with a more modest post at the King 2 square.

But in that case, what are the possibilities for developing the

Black Queen effectively? Actually, as you will discover during the course of the game, Black's Queen never moves from the first rank! As for Black's Queen Rook, it never moves at all.

These observations are important, for they show us the cause-and-effect sequence of bad development. Black's apparently trifling mistake at move 4 will continue to hound him for the remainder of this game.

Diagram 159

(Position after 6 N—B3)
To an experienced player, this position has all the earmarks of a lost game for Black, based on White's prospects of formidable attack later on.

As Black takes stock of the situation, he finds that White's advanced Pawn on the King 5 square is a thorn in his side. This Pawn has a cramping effect on Black's game, especially after he succeeds in castling. In that event, Black cannot play a piece to his King Bishop 3 square to guard his castled position.

Consequently, 6 ...... P—Q3 suggests itself here with a view to removing White's obnoxious King Pawn.

In that case, however, White simply increases his lead in development by playing 7 B—B4! (This in turn threatens 8 P×P, inflicting a weak isolated Queen Pawn—on an open file!—on Black.)

Therefore, after 6 ...... P—Q3; 7 B—B4 Black would most likely play 7 ...... P×P. Then, after 8 Q×Qch, N×Q; 9 B×KP, P—QB3; 10 Castles QR White continues to exert strong pressure on Black's unattractive position.

So, however Black plays, he is confronted with a choice of evils.

6 ......   B—K2

Black develops this Bishop modestly and prepares to castle. Sooner or later he must come to grips with the problem of developing his Queen Bishop, but in order to do this, he must move his Queen Pawn. (It is indicative of his difficulties that he never does get around to moving his Queen Pawn!)

7 N—Q5!   ......

A very interesting move, which on the face of it is a violation of the maxim that you ought not to move a piece twice in the opening.

However, there are times when we can violate the rule-of-thumb rules. In fact, there are times when we *should* violate them—and this is such a time!

In the first place, White's position is so superior that he can allow himself the luxury of wasting a move, if the worst comes to the worst. Actually, however, 7 N—Q5! is far from a wasted move. It centralizes the Knight on the Queen 5 square so powerfully and aggressively that the constricted situation of Black's pieces is greatly intensified.

Secondly, the position of the Knight at Queen 5 is full of latent menace. For example, Black is afraid to play 7 ...... P—Q3, for then comes 8 N×B, Q×N; 9 P×P and again Black is left with a weak isolated Pawn on the open Queen file.

7   ......   Castles ·

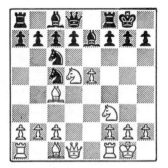

Diagram 160

(Position after 7 Castles)
White has come out of the opening with a far superior game.

Black castles his King into apparent safety—"apparent"

because White's lead in development and mobility provides the essential elements for a far-reaching and devastating attack.

| 8 | Castles | . . . . . . |

White's castling is qualitatively a horse of another color. To begin with, his King will be really safe—simply because Black, in his poorly developed state, does not have the slightest opportunity to attack the White King.

This realization is of the greatest value to us, demonstrating as it does that *without development there can be no attack.*

Castling is also of value to White because he can now put his King Rook to good use. Consider, for example, the possibility of playing KR—K1—K3—KN3——aiming directly at Black's King-side.

The White Rook maneuver we have just sketched out suggests still another thought. White's pieces occupy five ranks; Black's forces will soon occupy only three ranks. This dramatically sets off *White's considerable advantage in space.* This advantage gives his pieces more freedom of action and more maneuvering space.

Thus we perceive, with ever more clarifying detail, how White's superior development automatically creates possibilities for attack.

Black would like to free himself, but how?

If he plays 8 . . . . . . P—Q3, there follows 9 N×Bch, Q×N; 10 B—KN5! (developing free of charge), Q—Q2 (a miserable post for the Queen, blocking the development of Black's Queen Bishop); 11 P×P, P×P; 12 B—B4 and once more White has pressure on the weak isolated Queen Pawn.

| 8 | . . . . . . | N—K3 |

This at least prevents an eventual B—KN5 by White in the event of the disappearance of Black's King Bishop. But now this Knight has moved for the fourth time!

| 9 | P—B3 | . . . . . . |

White delays the development of his Queen Bishop for a more favorable opportunity (see this 12th move).

He plays the rather mysterious next move with a view to

driving off Black's Queen Knight with P—QN4—5, and also with the intention of posting his Queen powerfully at Queen Bishop 2. (From that square it will be aiming at Black's King-side.)

Now back to Black's problems. He is thinking hard about how to eliminate White's advanced King Pawn, which is stifling his position.

But 9 ...... P—Q3 will hardly do, for then comes 10 N×Bch, Q×N; 11 P×P, Q×P; 12 Q×Q, P×Q; 13 R—Q1 (White puts the newly liberated King Rook to good use on the open file, attacking the weak Pawn), N—K4; 14 B—K2, R—Q1; 15 P—QN3! followed by B—R3! with troublesome pressure on the isolated Queen Pawn.

Black understandably does not care for this line. But the alternative 9 ...... P—B3 has its drawbacks too: 10 N×Bch, Q×N; 11 P×P, Q×P; 12 N—N5, P—Q3; 13 Q—Q5, R—K1; 14 P—B4 and White has a fierce initiative.

> 9   ......   R—K1

Diagram 161

(Position after 9 ......
R—K1)
*Black contemplates a clumsy
rearranging maneuver: ......
B—B1 followed by ......
N—K2. But liberation is still
out of the question.*

> 10   P—QN4   ......

Continuing with his plan of dislodging Black's Queen Knight.

> 10   ......   B—B1

Spinelessly allowing White to drive off the Queen Knight. He should at least have played 10 ...... P—QR3 to maintain the position of his Queen Knight at Queen Bishop 3.

The retreat of the Bishop (backward development!) makes room for Black's Queen Knight at King 2. Black thinks of this as a benefit, in the sense that he will have more pieces on hand to guard his King. Actually he is wrong, as we shall see very quickly.

11   P—N5   ......

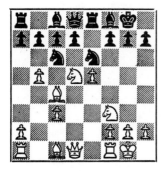

Diagram 162

(Position after 11 P—N5)
*Black's Queen Knight is driven
off to the King 2 square.
Result: Black's pieces are
jumbled together in a small area
and cannot function forcefully.*

Of course Black also has the possibility of playing 11 ...... N—R4. But then White simply plays 12 B—Q3 (aiming at Black's King-side) and the Knight is hopelessly stranded at the side of the board. Not an inviting prospect!

11   ......   N—K2
12   B—N5!   ......

At last the Bishop ventures forth, and its first move spells trouble for Black.

Diagram 163

(Position after 12 B—N5!)
*At first sight it seems that Black
can win a piece with 12 ......
N×B; 13 N×N/N5, N×N;
14 B×N, Q×N. How does
White meet this danger?*

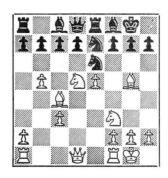

There is more in this position than meets the eye, for after

12 ...... N×B; 13 N×N/N5, N×N White plays 14 Q—R5! threatening 15 Q×RP mate. Black gets nowhere with 14 ...... N—B3 because of 15 P×N (remember what was said in the note to White's 5th move about the position of White's Pawn on the King 5 square?).

And if Black plays 14 ...... P—KR3 we get 15 Q×BPch, K—R1; 16 Q×N! winning on the spot because of the double threat of 17 Q—N8 mate and 17 N—B7ch winning Black's Queen.

If Black tries 12 ...... N×B; 13 N×N/N5, P—KR3 then White has 14 N×KBP!, K×N; 15 N×P dis ch followed by 16 N×QR with a won game.

Nor can Black try to free himself, for example 12 ...... P—QB3; 13 N×Nch, B×N; 14 B×B, Q×B; 15 Q—Q2 followed by 16 QR—Q1 with intolerable pressure on Black's backward Queen Pawn.

These drastic variations show graphically the dangers which now confront the Black King. Sooner or later White will blow up the castled position.

| 12 ...... | P—QN3 |

He must try to develop his Queen Bishop. But this does not help matters on the menaced King-side.

| 13 Q—B2! | ...... |

Nicely played. If now 13 ...... N×B; 14 N×N/N5 threatening mate and thus leaving Black no time to win a piece by ...... N×N.

At the same time this move, anticipating 13 ...... B—N2, makes room for White's Queen Rook at the Queen 1 square, pressing down relentlessly on Black's weakened Queen Pawn.

| 13 ...... | B—N2 |
| 14 QR—Q1 | Q—B1 |

Unpinning his Queen. However, these move-to-move measures cannot stave off the coming catastrophe on the King-side.

| 15 B×N! | ...... |

He sees through Black's despairing finesse: if 15 N×Nch,
B×N; 16 B×B, B×N! (Black's Queen, having moved, is not
attacked); 17 P×B, R×B and Black has gained a little freedom.

15	......	B×B

If 15 ...... B×N; 16 B/B4×B winning the Exchange.

16	N×Bch	R×N
17	N—R4!	......

White holds all the trumps. His pieces are trained on the
hostile King-side, while Black's forces are either ineffectual or
removed from that wing.

If Black tries 17 ...... P—N3 (to keep White's Knight out),
there follows 18 P—B4 followed by 19 P—B5 smashing up
Black's castled position.

17	......	R—K1

This is inevitable, in view of the coming N—B5. But the
Rook move does nothing to improve Black's prospects.

18	P—B4	Q—Q1
19	N—B5	N—B4

At last a glimmer of counterplay: Black threatens ......
B—K5.

20	KR—K1	......

White parries the threat by bringing a new piece into the
game. In addition, White's Rook move holds out the promise
of an eventual R—K3 followed by R—N3.

20	......	P—QR3

Attacking Two Knights' Defense ■ 123

Black tries to open lines on the Queen-side in the vain hope of diverting White from the main theater of war.

21 R—K3!   ......

The advance of this Rook to the third rank is ominous. If Black fully appreciates the point involved, he will play ...... R—KB1 to guard his vulnerable King Bishop 2 square, and thus prolong his resistance.

21 ......   P×P?

But Black misses the point.

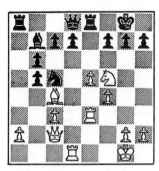

Diagram 165

(Position after 21 ......
P×P?)
White now has all the makings of a beautiful and conclusive sacrificial attack.

22 B×Pch!   ......

If Black disdains taking this obnoxious Bishop, he loses at least the Exchange, to begin with.

22 ......   K×B

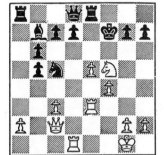

Diagram 166

(Position after 22 ......
K×B)
As so often happens in such positions, White proves the soundness of his first sacrifice by sacrificing a second piece.

Now the Black King is ringed about by powerful enemies, while his own forces merely twiddle their thumbs and do nothing to help him.

23   N—R6ch!!   . . . . . .

Even more unexpected than White's previous move.

However, there is sound method in White's seeming madness: if 23 . . . . . . P×N; 24 Q×Pch (the fulfillment of White's 13th move!), K—B1; 25 R—N3 and the powerful intervention of this Rook forces Black's downfall.

Even more striking, as an illustration of the power of White's King Pawn, is this possibility: 23 . . . . . . P×N; 24 Q×Pch, K—K3; 25 P—B5 mate!

23   . . . . . .   K—K2

The Black King tries to help himself by running away. It doesn't work; White's attack is overwhelming.

24   Q×P   . . . . . .

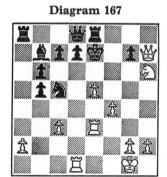

Diagram 167

(Position after 24 Q×P)
Black is helpless against White's threat of Q×Pch. Thus, 24 . . . . . . N—K3 is refuted by 25 P—B5, which not only attacks the Knight but "incidentally" threatens 26 P—B6ch, K—B1; 27 Q—N8 mate (or 27 Q—R8 mate).

How is Black to make room for his King?

The abject 24 . . . . . . Q—N1 suggests itself, but then there follows 25 N—B5ch, K—Q1; 26 Q—R4ch, K—B1; 27 N—K7ch, K—Q1 (if Black captures the Knight, White has a mate in two moves); 28 N—B6 dbl ch, K—B1; 29 Q—Q8ch!, R×Q; 30 N—K7 mate. A delightful finish, with Black's King blocked by his faithless allies.

24   . . . . . .   KR—N1

Black despair.

25   R—N3!   . . . . . .

Much stronger than the immediate N×Rch, as will become clear in the next note.

| 25 | ...... | Q—KB1 |
| 26 | N×Rch | ...... |

If now 26 ...... Q×N; 27 R×Pch wins Black's Queen.

| 26 | ...... | K—Q1 |
| 27 | R×NP | Q×P |

Black's resistance has crumpled.

| 28 | R/N7×Pch! | ...... |

So that if 28 ...... N×R; 29 Q×N mate.

| 28 | ...... | K—B1 |
| 29 | R—Q8 mate | |

Summary:

White's early lead in development (thanks to Black's faulty 4th move) enabled him to seize the initiative and gradually increase his command of the board. As the play continued, Black was unable to develop properly or find good squares for his pieces. By increasing the pressure, White obtained a position (see Diagram 163) which was bound to produce a win for him.

Such positions *must* be won by the aggressor. They can be won in various ways, depending on the inclinations and abilities of the player with the initiative. In this case, White headed consistently for King-side attack, and he saw his definitive opportunity in the position of Diagram 165.

The basic elements were there: (1) White had Queen, Rook, Knight, and Bishop poised for attack on the Black King; (2) Black's King had no support; (3) White's pieces were so powerfully posted that they were able to force checkmate on the Queen-side! Black's King could not escape from their clutches.

Think about this game before going on to the next lesson.

LESSON 7: PSYCHOLOGY
IN ATTACK AND DEFENSE

The knack of playing a forceful attack in chess is a skill that you can acquire and improve by studying model games in books. Acquiring that skill does not involve any special problems: you learn to play aggressive chess just as you learn to swim, type, or drive a car well.

There is, however, a wide chasm between studying an attack in a book and playing an attack in your own game. The actual game, as you experience it move by move, is full of excitement and emotional ups and downs. From the point of view of improving your chess skill it is of the greatest importance for you to be prepared, in your own play, for these emotional problems. Properly prepared, you can solve these problems convincingly. If you're not prepared, you're likely to lose many a won game.

You have heard repeatedly that chess is a game of rigorous logic; that chance plays no role in it; that only sheer intellect counts. Such ideas are misleading and unrealistic; they leave you unprepared for the personal elements that enter into every game of chess. When a stronger player is attacking against a weaker player, an objective analysis of the moves will not tell you the whole story.

A good many of these factors are illustrated in the following game. White is by far the better of the two players. Consequently he is prepared to take all sorts of headlong risks that he might well avoid against a stronger opponent.

Black knows very well that he's a weaker player, and so he is intimidated from the start. He is tense, timid, apologetically defensive.

White has not only an objective advantage based on superior playing ability: he has a *psychological* advantage as well. Black sees White's moves as being even stronger than they are; after all, he reasons, such a great player cannot make a mistake!

The result is that White goes in for a bit of bluffing. He makes moves that look more menacing than they are. The series of constant threats wears Black down. Eventually, in a position that is quite playable, he loses his head—and the game as well. The moral is that an attack—any attack—has a power that is greater over the board than it is in print.

To take such chances is a "calculated risk." You have to be very sure of yourself. You have to know your opponent's strong points and his limitations. Then the policy of calculated risk, judiciously applied, will win many an additional game for you. Fortune favors the brave—especially in chess.

But playing the defense requires courage too. Passive defense, conducted in a chicken-hearted spirit, rarely succeeds. Resourceful counterattack, or else a grim determination to see the crisis through, often beats back an offense that looks irresistible.

If you bear in mind these two paragraphs, you will see why White succeeds in this game and Black fails. White is buoyantly inventive—nothing discourages him. Black finds the going too hard—at a certain point he has had all the punishment he can take. Black's position collapses in the face of White's unrelenting threats.

RUY LOPEZ

	WHITE	BLACK
1	P—K4	P—K4
2	N—KB3	N—QB3

The reasoning behind these moves was explained in Lesson 6. But now White tries something new.

Diagram 168

(Position after 3 B—N5)
*This is the characteristic
position of the Ruy Lopez.*

3   B—N5   . . . . . .

A departure from the previous game, in which White played
3 B—B4.

The Bishop move here has some obvious values. It is a
developing move, and it prepares for castling.

In addition it involves a threat which may or may not
materialize. Under favorable circumstances White threatens to
play B×N followed by N×P winning a Pawn.

Right now, however, this is not a real threat. For example,
Black can challenge the Bishop with 3 . . . . . . P—QR3 and if
4 B×N, QP×B; 5 N×P, Black regains the Pawn at once
with the double attack 5 . . . . . . Q—Q5 or . . . . . . Q—N4.

It would be a great mistake, however, to despise 3 B—N5
because it does not involve a real threat. In many cases such
conditional threats are overlooked by the opponent. Then he
may make a move which allows the conditional threat to
become a real threat.

In other cases, the opponent may be aware of the conditional
threat. However, in the heat of the battle, preoccupied with
some other aspect of the position, he may momentarily forget
about the conditional threat: he may select a move which
makes the conditional threat operative.

Remember, also, that the conditional threat has a certain
psychological effect on the opponent. It puts him under pressure. Whatever move he has in mind, he must always check to
see whether it doesn't spoil his defense against the conditional

Ruy Lopez Attack ■ 129

threat. Thus the element of constraint serves to irritate him and put him in an uneasy frame of mind.

3 ...... N—KB3

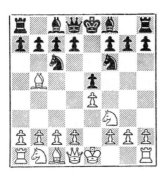

Diagram 169

(Position after 3 ......
N—KB3)
Black's last move is an excellent developing move that attacks White's King Pawn and also helps to prepare for castling.

Aside from any other virtues of 3 ...... N—KB3, it still maintains a satisfactory defense against White's conditional threat. For if now 4 B×N, QP×B; 5 N×P, Q—Q5 and Black regains the Pawn comfortably.

4 P—Q3 ......

Definitively protecting his King Pawn. The conditional threat has now become a real threat: 5 B×N, QP×B; 6 N×P and now Black can no longer regain the Pawn.

Therefore Black must give his King Pawn more solid protection.

4 ...... P—Q3

Now Black's King Pawn is securely guarded.

However, his last move has a theoretical drawback: his King Bishop is now hemmed in and has very little scope. (Note that White's King Bishop was not affected by his P—Q3, for his King Bishop had already been developed.)

5 P—KR3 ......

A strange-looking move, especially as theory frowns on such Rook Pawn moves as time-wasting and possibly weakening.

However, White has definite ideas in mind. First, he restrains the action of Black's Queen Bishop, as ...... B—N5 is ruled out.

Secondly, he wants to play B—K3 without having to reckon with ...... N—KN5, which might lead to an exchange of Knight for Bishop that would favor Black.

Third, White plans to castle rather late in the day, and on the Queen-side. Soon after Black castles, White will play P—KN4 in the hope of getting an attack against Black's castled King. This plan looks rather nebulous at the moment, but it will take on more concrete shape as the game progresses.

5 ......   P—KN3

Diagram 170

(Position after ...... P—KN3)

Rather than play the modest ...... B—K2, Black aims for ...... B—N2, which gives his pieces more playing room in the center and also enables the Bishop to bear down on the center squares.

The virtues of Black's fianchetto (...... P—KN3 followed by ...... B—N2) maneuver have been explained in the caption to Diagram 170. But this maneuver also has drawbacks, as we shall see a little later.

6   B—K3   B—N2

Diagram 171

(Position after 6 ...... B—N2)

White forms a plan to get rid of Black's valuable King Bishop. If White succeeds in this project, he can plot to establish his own pieces on the weakened black squares.

By playing 5 ...... P—KN3 Black created "holes" at his King Rook 3 and King Bishop 3 squares. (A "hole" in chess parlance refers to a square no longer protected by Pawns.)

While Black's King Knight Pawn was at its original square, it guarded Black's King Rook 3 and King Bishop 3 squares. Now that the Pawn has advanced, these squares must be guarded by Black's King Bishop, which moves on black squares.

7   Q—Q2   ......

And there we have it! White intends to play B—KR6, forcing the exchange of Black's valuable King Bishop.

Black can block this plan with 7 ...... P—KR3, but in that case he will be unable to castle—for that would lose his King Rook Pawn.

(Note, by the way, that thanks to 5 P—KR3 Black need not reckon with the possibility of ...... N—KN5, a move that would spoil his plan if the Knight move were feasible.)

7   ......   Castles

Black decides to castle, come what may.

To an inexperienced player it is not immediately obvious that Black's castled position has been weakened, and that it contains a target for White's attack.

The target is Black's King Knight Pawn. White's grand plan is to play P—KR4 followed by P—R5, forcing the opening of the King Rook file. The second step will be to utilize the open King Rook file for attack on Black's King.

This is a far-reaching plan which, as you will see, requires considerable preparation. But if White keeps this plan in mind, it will guide him to certain moves. For example, since he knows that he wants to keep his King Rook on the King Rook file, he avoids castling on that wing. Thus, even at this early stage, White knows that he will eventually castle on the Queen-side. This will enable him to swing his Queen Rook over to the King-side to take part in the attack. (See White's 18th move.)

8   B—KR6   ......

Forcing the elimination of Black's black-squared Bishop, as per plan.

A good idea here for Black is 8 ...... N—K1 (intending counterplay with ......P—B4). If then 9 P—KN4, there might follow 9 ...... P—B4!; 10 NP×P, P×P and Black threatens to win a Pawn with ...... P×P. Despite the opening of the King Knight file (exposing his King to possible attack), Black would stand well because his pieces would have a great deal of playing room.

But Black is too timid, and consequently he soon finds himself in trouble.

8 ......   N—KR4

A colorless move which gets Black nowhere. Knights are almost invariably badly placed at the side of the board.

Black is playing for a little trap: if now 9 P—KN4, N—B5!; 10 B/R6×N, P×B; 11 Q×P??, B×QNP and Black wins the White Rook. But White avoids this premature advance, and simply reserves P—KN4 for a more suitable time.

9 N—B3   ......

Now White threatens 10 P—KN4, for if 10 ...... N—B5?; 11 B/R6×N, P×B; 12 Q×P as 12 ...... B×QNP is no longer feasible.

Even now 9 ...... P—B4 would be worth considering, but Black chooses a different idea.

9 ......   N—K2

(Position after 9 ... N—K2)
Black plans to play...P—QB3 followed by ... P—Q4 when that move becomes feasible. If Black can take a powerful stand in the center by these moves, he can neutralize the force of White's coming attack.

Diagram 172

10   P—Q4!

Splendidly alert play!

Rather than allow Black to take the initiative in the center, White advances first, postponing P—KN4 for a while. He sees that on 10 . . . . . . P×P; 11 N×P his forces will acquire greater freedom of action, and the coming P—KN4 will drive Black's Knight back with gain of time.

            10   . . . . . .   P—QB3

A crafty move. Black hopes for the thoughtless reply 11 B—R4? allowing 11 . . . . . . P—QN4; 12 B—N3, P×P; 13 N×P, P—N5!; 14 N—Q1 (a poor spot for the Knight, but 14 QN—K2 is answered by 14 . . . . . . P—QB4!; 15 N—KB3, B×NP!), P—QB4!; 15 N—KB3, B—N2 with a terrific initiative for Black.

Diagram 173

(Position after 10 . . . . . .
P—QB3)
*White's choice of a retreat for
his King Bishop is crucial.*

            11   B—K2!   . . . . . .

Another fine move which crushes Black's hopes. If now 11 . . . . . . P×P; 12 N×P gains time by threatening B×N with complete smash-up of Black's castled position.

Meanwhile White threatens 12 B×B followed by 13 P×P winning a Pawn.

            11   . . . . . .   Q—B2

This protects the Pawn, though with proper play White can win the Pawn anyway. But proper timing is of the essence—if 12 P×P, P×P; 13 P—KN4, N—B5! and Black stands well (his Knight is additionally guarded by his Queen).

12　P—KN4!　　　......

Another fine move. Black cannot play 12 ...... N—B5? which would now lose a Pawn because Black's Queen does not aid in the protection of the Knight. (That protection would only come into effect after 12 P×P.)

12　......　　　N—B3

This inglorious retreat is forced, under the circumstances.

13　P×P　　　　......

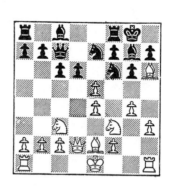

Diagram 174

(Position after 13 P×P)
Interestingly enough, White is in a position to win a Pawn by force.

13　......　　　P×P

White can now win a Pawn by 14 B×B, K×B; 15 Q—N5! as 15 ...... N—Q2? is impossible because of 16 Q×N.

After 14 B×B, K×B; 15 Q—N5! Black can try a little swindle: 15 ...... R—K1; 16 Q×KP, Q×Q; 17 N×Q, N/K2—N1; 18 P—B4 (forced, if he is to retain the extra Pawn), N×KP?; 19 N×N, P—B3. Now it looks as if White must lose back a Knight, but he has the winning reply 20 N—Q6! If then 20 ...... R—K3; 21 N×B?, P×N! is good for Black, as the White Knight is trapped!

However, on 20 ...... R—K3 White plays 21 N/K5—B7! maintaining his material advantage.

This variation is worth your studying with some care, for it shows how a "simple" win of material can often be brought about only by the most careful and precise tactical play.

14　Q—N5!?　　　......

But White has other ideas. He gives Black a chance to save

his Pawn, but only at the cost of playing 14 ...... B×B, allowing White's Queen to take up a vicious attacking post at the hole King Rook 6. Here the Queen, supported by a later N—KN5, will occupy a menacing post and make life exceedingly hazardous for Black's King.

Yet, as the future play will prove, only the greatest ingenuity can keep White's attack going, and even with White's best play—real grandmaster chess—Black will still have adequate defenses!

Objectively viewed, then, White's best was 14 B×B, K×B; 15 Q—N5 winning a Pawn. But White, confident of his superior ability, does not want a long, "dreary" endgame. He wants to win quickly by brilliant attack. And so he chooses the *objectively weaker line*, with sanguine hopes of battering his opponent into submission. His judgment, based on *psychological* considerations, proves correct. He expects his opponent to crack up—and his opponent obligingly does just that.

14 ...... B×B

The only way to save the Pawn. But now White's Queen takes up a powerful post on the King Rook 6 square.

15 Q×B Q—Q3

Black protects his Queen Knight so that he can answer 16 Q—N5 with 16 ...... N—Q2, safely guarding his King Pawn.

There is another point to ...... Q—Q3. As we know, White wants to castle Queen-side in order to get his Queen Rook into the attack with QR—KN1. But with Black's Queen stationed where it is, the White King cannot pass over his Queen 1 square for castling.

This explains White's reply.

16 B—Q3 ......

White blocks the action of Black's Queen on the Queen file, thus making castling on the Queen-side feasible.

16 ...... P—QN4

A futile gesture of counterattack which has no effect on the course of the game. At least 16 ...... B—K3 would help complete Black's development.

Diagram 175

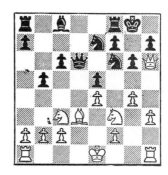

(Position after 16 ......
P—QN4)
White is now ready to castle on the Queen-side, after which his attack will develop in real earnest.

17   Castles QR   ......

Suddenly White's Queen Rook is on the point of taking part in the attack!

17   ......   Q—B4

Perhaps Black is afraid of 18 B×P (attacking Black's Queen). This may or may not be a threat, as it would lead to the opening of the Queen Knight file, on which Black could post his Rooks and Queen for attack against White's King.

But here we see a vivid contrast in the basic attitudes of the two players: aggressive, speculative thinking is quite congenial to White, who disdains a Pawn or two if he sees even a vague opportunity of tearing his opponent limb from limb. Black, on the other hand, is timid, skeptical, and colorless in his approach to the problems of attack and defense. This fundamental difference expresses itself in the following play, which White handles incisively while Black fumbles.

18   QR—N1!   ......

An important prelude to the intended advance P—KR4 followed by P—R5.

Note that White has consistently avoided P—N5?, which would be answered by ...... N—R4. In that case it would be very difficult for White to force open a file on the King-side.

And there would be other drawbacks: White would be unable to play the menacing N—N5, and finally his Queen would be cut off from the other White forces and could only make her way back with great effort and several time-wasting moves.

For all these reasons, P—N5? would be quite inferior. This is a useful point to study, as the same possibility turns up often in similar situations.

Meanwhile, we observe that Black has attacked White's King Bishop Pawn and White has calmly ignored the attack. Is White bluffing, or does he really have some hidden though perfectly valid refutation?

As it happens, White does have a crushing reply to 18 ...... Q×P?, namely 19 R—B1, Q—B4; 20 N—N5!, Q—Q3; 21 R×N, Q×R; 22 Q×RP mate.

| 18 ...... | B—K3 |

Finally developing this Bishop, Black establishes communication between his Rooks—an important point.

| 19 P—KR4! | ...... |

Now the tension increases move by move, as White creates more serious problems for his opponent to solve.

Diagram 176

(Position after 19 P—KR4!)
Now White offers a Pawn in three different ways. Is all this sound?

Can Black accept any of the Pawn sacrifices? Let's see:

Suppose Black tries 19 ...... N×NP? Then we get 20 R×N!, B×R; 21 N—N5 followed by Q×RP mate.

Suppose Black tries 19 ...... Q×BP? In that event, it will

not do for White to reply 20 R—B1, for then Black has
20 . . . . . . N×NP! (White's King Knight Pawn is unprotected!)
and if 21 Q—N5 (*looks* devastating), Black has 21 . . . . . .
Q—K6ch forcing the exchange of Queens with an easy endgame win. Or if 21 Q×Rch, R×Q; 22 R×Q, N×R with the
same result.

Does all this mean, then, that Black can play 19 . . . . . .
Q×BP? with satisfactory results? No, it does not. For after
19 . . . . . . Q×BP? White has 20 N—N5! (threatening R—B1).
If then 20 . . . . . . K—R1; 21 R—B1, Q—K6ch; 22 K—N1,
N/K2—N1 (apparently trapping White's Queen), there follows
the crushing 23 N×BPch winning Black's Queen! Or if 21
. . . . . . N/K2—N1; 22 R×Q, N×Q; 23 R×N winning a piece.

In all these variations, and in the play to come, we see how
dangerously Black has weakened himself by . . . . . . P—KN3
and the following disappearance of his King Bishop.

Nevertheless, *if Black defends himself with determination*, he
can survive the attack! White has assets for attack, but they do
not win automatically. Black has defensive assets too. It is the
interplay of assets and liabilities that makes chess the great
fighting game it is. But Black must fight!

>19 . . . . . .   B×NP!

This capture is playable. Has White overplayed his hand?

>20 N—N5!   . . . . . .

Threatening 21 R×B and wins, as Black's Knight on the
King Bishop 3 square is tied to the defense.

If Black tries 20 . . . . . . B—R4 (temporarily blocking the
line-opening procedure), White has 21 B—K2! eliminating the
hostile Bishop, after which the deadly P—R5 is again
threatened.

>20 . . . . . .   K—R1!

Well played! Suddenly Black threatens 21 . . . . . . N/K2—
N1!! (not 21 . . . . . . N/B3—N1??; 22 Q×RP mate) and White

can save his trapped Queen only by playing 22 N×BPch, which leaves him a piece down.

This explains why 21 R×B? will not do, for after 21 ...... N/K2—N1!; 22 N×BPch, R×N; 23 Q—N5, N×R White has no compensation for having lost the Exchange.

But White keeps the attack alive with an amazing resource:

21 N×RP!!   ......

Beautiful play.

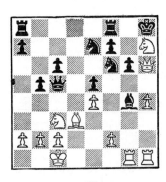

Diagram 177

(Position after 21 N×RP!!)
*White threatens to checkmate
on the move: 22 N×N mate!
How does Black defend?*

21 ......   N/K2—N1!

Attacking the White Queen, Black parries the mate threat.

22 Q—N5   ......

White does not fear 22 ...... N×N in reply, for then comes 23 Q×B regaining the sacrificed piece.

(It is remarkable, by the way, that White's attack has generated so much power without the assistance of his Knight and Bishop. This seeming paradox is explained by the fact that White's Rooks are full of menacing potentialities, while Black's Rooks are idle.)

22 ......   K×N

Here is a point at which the average player would be stymied. White is a clear piece down, and Black seems quite safe.

How should White proceed? It will not do to play 23 R×B, N×R; 24 Q×N—leaving Black the material advantage of the Exchange ahead.

23 P—R5!   ......

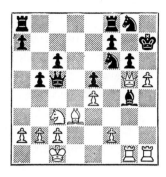

Diagram 178

(Position after 23 P—R5!)
At last White has arrived at his cherished goal of forcing open the King Rook file for a decisive attack.

White's immediate threat is 24 P×P dbl ch, K—N2; 25 R—R7ch! N×R; 26 P×N dis ch, K×P; 27 R—R1ch, B—R4; 28 R×Bch, N—R3; 29 R×N mate. This drastic variation is a perfect example of the kind of attack White has been seeking from the very start.

Black has three ways of capturing the King Rook Pawn— and capture it he must. But which way?

There is nothing in 23 ...... N×RP, for then comes 24 R×B! (not 24 Q×B, N/N1—B3!) and now Black is helpless against the coming 25 R×Nch, P×R; 26 Q—N7 mate.

So, after 23 ...... N×RP; 24 R×B! Black cannot play 24 ...... N—R3 because of 25 R×N—nor can he play 24 ...... N/N1—B3 because of 25 Q×N/B6.

Coming back to the position of Diagram 178, we see that 23 ...... P×P is even less inviting because of 24 P—B3. This wins Black's Bishop, which cannot retreat because of the reply 25 Q—N7 mate.

Thus, after 23 ...... P×P; 24 P—B3 White would regain the sacrificed material and his attack would continue in high gear.

Black finds the only playable move.

      23   ......   B×P

Now White loses with 24 R×Bch? as Black has 24 ...... N×R in reply (of course not 24 ...... P×R?? which allows 25 Q—N7 mate in reply).

24 B—K2!   ......

The right way to continue the attack: he takes advantage of the pin on Black's Bishop.

If now 24 ...... K—N2; 25 B×B, N×B; 26 Q×N and White has regained the sacrificed material and threatens Q—R8 mate.

Since Black must return the extra piece in any event, he moves his King Rook to give his King a flight square in case of need.

24 ......   KR—Q1
25 B×B   ......

The Bishop is immune from 25 ...... P×B?? for then comes 26 Q—N7 mate.

However, White threatens 26 B×P dbl ch, K—N2; 27 B—R5 dis ch (another way is 27 B—R7 dis ch etc.), K—B1; 28 Q—N7ch, K—K2; 29 Q×Pch, K—Q3; 30 R—Q1ch etc.

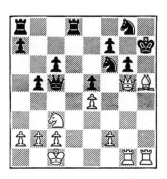

Diagram 179

(Position after 25 B×B)
Despite White's threatening position, Black can still put up an adequate resistance.

25 ......   N×B
26 R×Nch   ......

Again we have our familiar theme: if 26 ...... P×R??; 27 Q—N7 mate.

Now the worst is over for Black. Despite the terrific battering he has been taking, simplification has been going on steadily and White has accomplished very little with all his ingenuity!

26 ......   K—N2
27 Q—R4   ......

142 ■ Lesson 7—Psychology

White threatens to keep up the attack with R—R8. Black parries by bringing out his Knight.

27 ..... N—B3

Diagram 180

(Position after 27 .....
N—B3)
White's attack has pretty much petered out and he is still a Pawn down.

28 R—B5 ......

Threatening to capture the Knight, but Black has several obvious defenses.

28 ..... Q—Q3

Judging by what happens on the next move, 28 ......
Q—K2 was a bit safer. But the text move is quite playable.

29 P—B4!? ......

This is about all that White has left in the way of keeping up the attack.

Black should now play 29 ...... R—K1! If then 30 Q—N5, N—Q2 is adequate—or even 30 ...... N—R2!

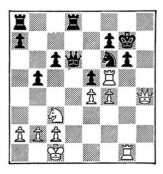

Diagram 181

(Position after 29 P—B4!?)
At last Black has an easy defense—which he well deserves after all that he's been through.

In that event, White's attack would be stopped in its tracks, and he would remain a Pawn down, with considerable likelihood of losing! So here we have an instructive situation, which brings us back to White's fateful 14th move. If White had played 14 B×B, K×B; 15 Q—N5, he would have won a Pawn with a winning endgame. Instead he chose an inordinately difficult middle game which might well have lost the game for him. Thus it seems the Day of Judgment has arrived for White.

29 ......   P×P??

Loses by force.

The likely explanation of this mistake is that the game was played under a time limit of 30 moves in two hours. The chances are that Black was very short of time and had to move hastily.

As previously explained, 29 ...... R—K1! holds the position satisfactorily.

30 P—K5   Q—Q7ch

Thus Black avoids losing the piece. This is a triumph of a sort, but very a short-lived one. For now *Black's Queen has been bodily removed from the scene of action*—with disastrous consequences that will be felt at once.

31 K—N1   ......

Diagram 182

(Position after 31 K—N1)
Black must now move his attacked Knight, after which pandemonium breaks loose.

31 ......   N—Q4

If anything, 31 ...... N—Q2 is even worse, for then comes 32 P—K6!, P×P; 33 Q—K7ch and wins. Or White can win with the same brilliant sacrifice that he employs in the text.

32 R×BPch!!   ......

Diagram 183

(Position after 32 R×BPch!!)
*White's brilliant sacrifice opens
up the position for a quickly
decisive attack.*

This brutal move leaves Black no choice, for if 32 ......
K—N1? White has 33 Q—R7 mate. After the forced acceptance
of the sacrifice Black will be a Rook ahead—yet he will have a
totally lost game, thanks to the exposed position of his King
and the lack of support from his other pieces—especially
his Queen.

But there is another moral to this position. With White's
material minus, nothing less than such a daring sacrifice can
turn the situation to his advantage. A prosaic continuation
would not be good enough to achieve success.

$$32 \quad ...... \qquad\qquad K \times R$$
$$33 \quad Q—R7ch \qquad\qquad ......$$

The indicated follow-up. White penetrates ruthlessly into the
heart of Black's position.

If now 33 ...... K—K3; 34 R×Pch, K×P; 35 Q—KN7ch,
K—B4; 36 R—N5ch, K—K3; 37 R—K5ch, K—Q3; 38
N—K4 mate.

Or if 33 ...... K—B1; 34 P—K6! (but not 34 R×P??,
Q—K8ch forcing mate!), N×Nch; 35 P×N, R—Q2 (else 35
Q—KB7 mate); 36 P×R, R—Q1; 37 R×P with irresistible
mating threats.

$$33 \quad ...... \qquad\qquad K—K1$$
$$34 \quad P—K6 \qquad\qquad ......$$

Threatening 35 Q—KB7 mate. And Black's Queen can do
nothing about the threat!

Ruy Lopez Attack ■ 145

34	......	N × Nch
35	P × N	......

If now 35 ...... R—Q2; 36 P × Rch, Q × P; 37 Q—N8ch (or Q—R8ch) winning Black's Rook.

35	......	R—Q5

Pathetically hoping for 36 P × R?, Q—N5ch; 37 K—R1, Q—B6ch; 38 K—N1, Q—N5ch; 39 K—B1, Q—R6ch; 40 K—Q1, Q—KB6ch; 41 K—Q2, Q—K6ch and White cannot escape from the perpetual check!

But White, at last in sight of victory, has no intention of snapping up the unwanted Rook.

36	Q—KB7ch	......

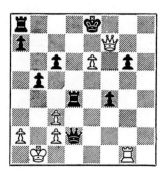

Diagram 184

(Position after 36 Q—KB7ch)
White can now force the queening of his King Pawn—and with check!

36	......	K—Q1
37	P—K7ch	K—B2

Or 37 ...... K—Q2; 38 P—K8/Q dbl ch!

38	P—K8/Q dis ch	......

Black can resign without a qualm.

38	......	K—N3
39	Q × R	Resigns

Summary:

White played for attack from the very beginning. He wanted to attack whether the position was suitable or not. Logically dangerous, his decision was psychologically sound. Knowing that he was the better player, he realized that he could take liberties.

The fate of this game hinged on two crises: White's objectively incorrect 14th move, and Black's collapse on move 29.

The great lesson to be learned from this game is that determination and fighting spirit can often carry out a faulty plan successfully. Don't ignore the personal factor!

LESSON 8:

CUMULATIVE BUILD-UP

OF A CRUSHING ATTACK

Nothing is more enjoyable in chess than to carry out a brilliant, slashing attack full of scintillating sacrifices and stunning surprise moves. But such an attack does not arise out of nothing. It must be formed in a favorable position under favorable circumstances.

In the following extraordinarily brilliant game, for example, the brilliancies do not start until the game is three-quarters over. Yet the brilliant part is what impresses us—the part that we never forget.

This is natural and quite common, but it is also illusory. Recognizing the interrelation between strategy and tactics is one of the steps toward becoming a good player. We start with a perfectly even position, yet in order to carry out a successful attack, we have to arrive at some imbalance. It is this imbalance which makes it possible to succeed.

How does this imbalance come into existence? At the start, both players have their pieces equally well posted. Once the struggle starts and progresses, one player posts his pieces well, the other posts his badly. The result is that the opening equilibrium has disappeared. The first player has an advantage.

Or perhaps the first player avoids any possible loss of time. The second player dawdles, or repeats moves with the same pieces. Again the opening equilibrium has been disturbed; the first player has an advantage.

Perhaps the second player has created serious weaknesses in his position. Perhaps he has exposed his King to attack. Here too the opening equilibrium has been disturbed—and in the most critical way possible.

When the imbalance is very noticeable, when the resulting advantage is very great, the chances are that a winning attack is possible. *For an attack is nothing but a concerted attempt to impose one's will on the enemy.* The player with the advantage sets himself a goal: to checkmate the hostile King, to win material, to force a decisive weakness, to simplify into a won endgame, and the like. If his advantage is big enough and he knows how to apply it properly, his attack will succeed.

Strictly speaking, there are no "surprise moves" in an attack. That the player with the advantage can unleash moves of enormous striking power, stands to reason. The bigger his advantage, the more powerful his attacking thrusts. *It is we who are surprised because we have not fully appraised the extent of the advantage that makes the powerful moves possible.*

Sacrifices—that is, giving up units of greater value for units of lesser value—are also a logical feature of the attack. In this game Black repeatedly offers sacrifices because their acceptance will allow other units—academically weaker units—to operate with more than usual force. And why do they operate with more than usual force?—because of the previously obtained advantage which has enhanced their striking force.

In playing over the following game, then, notice how Black, for the first 30 moves or so, patiently builds up an advantage that will store potential power for a violent attack later on. And when that attack comes, you realize that it is the logical sequel to the previous preparatory process of acquiring a positional advantage.

QUEEN'S GAMBIT DECLINED

WHITE	BLACK
1 P—Q4	P—Q4

This is a different type of opening from the ones we have encountered in the earlier part of this book. It leads generally to a "close" game with more maneuvering possibilities than we get after 1 P—K4. This puts a premium on each player's foresight and planning abilities.

| 2 N—KB3 | ...... |

In Queen Pawn openings both sides aim to control the important central King 5 square with the King Knight.

| 2 ...... | N—KB3 |
| 3 P—B4 | ...... |

White offers a gambit in the hope of removing Black's Queen Pawn from its Queen 4 square. If Black plays 3 ...... P×P, White hopes to establish a broad Pawn center in due course with P—K4.

| 3 ...... | P—K3 |

This maintains Black's hold on the center by supporting his Queen Pawn. (We need not linger very long on 3 ...... P×P, as White can recover the Pawn by 4 Q—R4ch—or by 4 P—K3, P—QN4; 5 P—QR4, P—B3; 6 P—QN3!, and White regains the Pawn advantageously.)

| 4 N—B3 | QN—Q2 |

Here ...... N—B3? would be poor play, because in this opening Black must be ready sooner or later to play ...... P—QB4, and the development of the Knight to Queen Bishop 3 would block this plan. (White would be able to operate on the Queen Bishop file—a maneuver Black would be unable to imitate, with his Queen Bishop Pawn blocked on its original square.)

| 5 B—N5 | ...... |

The most aggressive development for this Bishop.

5 . . . . . .   P—B3

Giving further protection to his Queen Pawn, and also having in view a counterattack by . . . . . . Q—R4, pinning White's Queen Knight.

6   P—K3   . . . . . .

White provides definitive protection for his Queen Bishop Pawn and also prepares for the development of his King Bishop.

6   . . . . . .   Q—R4

Diagram 185

(Position after 6 . . . . . . Q—R4)
Black's pinning move is well timed, for now that White has played 6 P—K3, his Queen Bishop cannot return to Queen 2 to unpin his Queen Knight.

This line of play is known as the Cambridge Springs Variation. Many an inexperienced player has been caught in the toils of its numerous traps.

Suppose, for example, that White unthinkingly plays 7 B—Q3, P×P; 8 B×BP? Then comes 8 . . . . . . N—K5! with double attack on White's exposed Queen Bishop and on his pinned Knight. This attack will cost White a Pawn at the very least.

7   B×N   . . . . . .

White avoids trouble by immediately getting rid of his Queen Bishop, thus ruling out any trappy double attack by . . . . . . N—K5.

7   . . . . . .   N×B

Black now has two Bishops against Bishop and Knight. To have the Bishop-pair is considered a positional advantage. Why?

As far as this position is concerned, it is not easy to explain.

Black's King Bishop has a good diagonal, to be sure, but his other Bishop—the Queen Bishop—has little scope. This Bishop travels on white squares, and the presence of Black's King Pawn and Queen Bishop Pawn on white squares reduces the mobility of his Queen Bishop to next to nothing.

But suppose that later on Black is able to give his Queen Bishop more scope by playing ...... P—K4 or ...... P—QB4 or perhaps even both moves. Once these Pawns have moved off white squares, Black's Queen Bishop will have greatly increased freedom of action. In that case, both Black Bishops will have considerable scope and much of the board will come under their jurisdiction.

Now contrast the long cruising range of the Bishops—at their ideal best—with the short hops of the Knight. Actually the Knight—any Knight—is quite vulnerable against judicious Pawn moves by the opponent, which cut off valuable squares from the Knight's range. (Note that later on, when White plays 25 N—R4, intending N—B5, Black replies 25 ...... P—N3, preventing White from playing the intended Knight move.)

So, to sum up, this is what often happens in the struggle between two Bishops on one side, and Bishop and Knight on the other side: the two Bishops increase their command of the board steadily, while at the same time the lone Knight's mobility is cut down by the opponent's adoption of the right kind of Pawn moves.

How this struggle actually works out in a real game will be seen in the following play. Here the struggle goes hand in hand with another process: Black's steady accumulation of small positional advantages which finally add up to a big plus. This big plus makes possible the strikingly brilliant attack which winds up the game.

As you study the unfolding of this game, one important facet will stand out: *as the power of Black's Bishops increases, his general advantage increases. And when his powerful attack gets under way, his Bishops play a prominent role.* So, keep your eye on those Bishops!

      8   P—QR3   . . . . . .

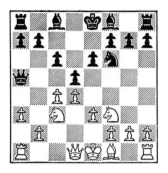

Diagram 186

(Position after 8 P—QR3)
White's last move rules out the pinning maneuver . . . . . .
B—N5. Nevertheless, Black still manages to make good use of the pin by the Queen.

      8   . . . . . .   N—K5

Black wants to free his slightly cramped position, and one of the best ways to accomplish this is to do a bit of exchanging. Momentarily Black threatens to win a Pawn, but White can defend himself against the threat in various ways.

To be sure, some of these ways are better than others. For example, 9 Q—B2 will not do because then comes 9 . . . . . . B—N5 (White's Queen Rook Pawn is pinned!); 10 R—B1 (else White loses a Pawn), B×Nch; 11 P×B, Q×RP and Black has won a Pawn after all.

      9   Q—N3   . . . . . .

White guards his Knight and also prevents . . . . . . B—N5.

      9   . . . . . .   B—K2

The Bishop is developed modestly enough, and there is nothing very impressive about the power of Black's Bishops *at this point.* It is their *potential power* that matters.

      10   B—Q3   . . . . . .

White develops his Bishop, and at the same time prepares to challenge the position of Black's advanced Knight. If now 10 . . . . . . Castles; 11 Castles KR, and Black must decide what

Crushing Attack ■ 153

to do with his Knight. If he retreats 11 ...... N—B3, he has lost valuable time.

If he supports the venturesome Knight with 11 ...... P—KB4, he creates a "hole" at his King 4 square which can become a serious weakness.

The best solution seems to be an exchange of Knights, so Black plays it at once.

10	......	N × N

Now, if White is so minded, he can play for the exchange of Queens by 11 Q × N, Q × Qch; 12 P × Q. But after 12 ...... P × P; 13 B × BP etc., Black's Bishops would begin to play their important endgame role from the very start for the simplified stage of the endgame is the special domain of the Bishops. At that point they can exert their sway, with only slight chance of counterattack or diversion by the enemy.

11	P × N	......

White prefers to seek his chances in the more complex ramifications of the middle game.

11	......	P × P

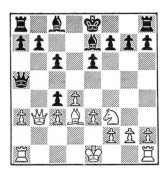

Diagram 187

(Position after 11 ......
P × P)
Black's exchange of Pawns plays an important role in his plan of the game.

By playing ...... P × P Black "gives up the center"—that is, he gives up his foothold in the center. His Queen Pawn disappears, and the road is cleared for White's P—K4.

But Black is well aware of what he wants: he intends to

play . . . . . B—B3 followed by . . . . . . P—K4 getting a new foothold in the center.

If White plays accurately, he can foil this plan—but Black will obtain compensation in another form.

12 B×BP   . . . . . .

This is a difficult position for an inexperienced player to appraise. White is ready to take up an imposing position in the center with P—K4. His Bishop and Queen are strongly placed on the same diagonal. His Knight has access to the important center square King 5.

And yet the future lies with Black—because of his Bishops!

12 . . . . . .   B—B3!

After the routine 12 . . . . . . Castles White could play 13 N—K5, B—B3; 14 P—B4! In that case, ... B×N would be poor play because White would recapture with his King Bishop Pawn, gaining the open King Bishop file for his pieces. And of course . . . . . . B×N would be the end of Black's Bishop-pair.

So Black avoids all these difficulties with the alert Bishop move.

White, to be sure, can now proceed with 13 P—K4, Castles; 14 P—K5, B—K2; 15 Castles KR. But then Black plays 15 . . . . . . P—QB4! with pressure on White's Pawn center, and follows up with . . . . . . P—QN3 and . . . . . . B—N2 giving his Queen Bishop a magnificent diagonal.

If White does not care for this prospect, he can answer 15 . . . . . . P—QB4! with 16 P—Q5, P×P; 17 B×P, R—N1; 18 P—B4. But then Black's Queen Bishop is at last free, making 18 . . . . . . B—B4 or 18 . . . . . . B—N5 possible.

In either case we would have a position full of fight, with chances for both sides.

13 Castles KR   . . . . . .

This somewhat slower line indicates a policy of drift which can do White no good in the long run.

13 . . . . . .   Castles

A necessary preliminary for ...... P—K4, which cannot be played at once due to the reply B×Pch.

            14   P—K4   P—K4!

Compare this position with the ones described in the note to Black's 12th move. Black has organized counterplay in the center, even at the "risk" of seeing one of his Bishops disappear after 15 P×P, B×P; 16 N×B, Q×N.

This line would leave Black with a Queen-side majority of Pawns—three Pawns to two—with a notable advantage for the eventual endgame. There might follow 17 QR—K1 (intending P—B4), P—QN4!; 18 B—Q3, B—K3; 19 Q—B2, KR—Q1 with a splendid game for Black, as 20 P—KB4? is premature because of 20 ...... Q—QB4ch followed by 21 ...... Q×RP.

            15   P—Q5   ......

There *seems* to be more fight in 15 QR—K1, momentarily leaving the center Pawns intact; but in that case Black has a fighting reply in 15 ...... B—N5!; 16 Q×P, B×N; 17 P×B, P×P etc. What is suspicious about the text is that with White Pawns on the white squares King 4 and Queen 5, White's Bishop has been deprived of considerable mobility. And since the Knight already has little scope, White's prospects look none too promising.

            15   ......   Q—B2

Black directs his Queen more toward the center and also guards his Queen Knight Pawn so that he can try to develop his Queen Bishop.

            16   B—Q3   ......
            16   ......   P—QN3

Black prepares to fianchetto his Queen Bishop. Slowly but steadily he goes on with his development, while White drifts. White's trouble is that his previous inexact moves have debarred him from forming good plans at this point.

Diagram 188

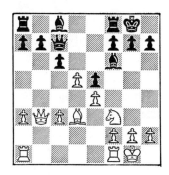

(Position after 16 B—Q3)
White prepares for P—B4,
which will solidify the support
of his Queen Pawn. It will
also complete the burial of his
Bishop.

      17   P—B4   . . . . . .

Now White's Bishop is blocked by White Pawns at Queen
Bishop 4, Queen 5, and King 4.

      17   . . . . . .   B—N2

At the moment this Bishop's future doesn't look very bright,
as it is blocked by its own Pawn. However, it has splendid
prospects at Queen Rook 3, or even back at its original square
once Black has placed his Queen Rook in good play with . . . . . .
QR—Q1.

      18   KR—B1   . . . . . .

With the transparent hope of playing P—B5. But nothing
comes of it, although White is doubtless disappointed. He
hopes for 18 . . . . . . P—B4? which would wall in Black's King
Bishop and leave it with very little scope.

      18   . . . . . .   B—K2!

Diagram 189

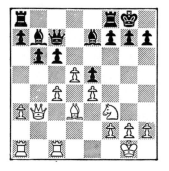

(Position after 18 . . . . . .
B—K2!)
Black prevents P—B5 (which
would have given White some
play on the Queen-side), and
prepares to post his King
Bishop at the magnificent
square Queen Bishop 4.

19 R—B2   ......

A better course is 19 Q—N2 and if 19 ...... P—B3; 20 N—Q2 in order to answer 20 ...... B—B4 with 21 N—N3.

        19 ......   B—B4

Here the Bishop is trained on White's King-side, with extremely unpleasant consequences for White.

        20 Q—N2   ......

Now, as will be seen, this maneuver is not so effective as it would have been earlier.

        20 ......   P—B3

Note that White cannot play 21 N—Q2? because of 21 ...... B—Q5.

        21 R—N1   ......

He removes his Rook from the dangerous diagonal.

        21 ......   QR—Q1

Now this Rook is ready to take part in the King-side attack which Black is gradually preparing.

        22 P—QR4   ......

Hoping for P—R5, but Black prevents the move easily enough. Nor does N—Q2—N3 look very promising here, as it would remove the Knight from the defense of White's King-side.

        22 ......   B—R3!

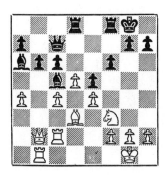

Diagram 190

(Position after 22 ...... B—R3!)
After Black's last move, he can answer 23 P—R5 with NP×P.

        23 R—Q1   ......

By now it has become clear that White is "swimming." He has no convincing continuation, and must await the unfolding of Black's plans.

23 ...... KR—K1

As the game goes, this turns out to be a very valuable move.

24 Q—N3 ......

White has been deprived of any constructive possibilities.

24 ...... R—Q3!

The move of a master. Black foresees that this Rook will eventually be able to swing over to the King-side.

25 N—R4 ......

Hoping, rather innocently, to be able to play N—B5.

25 ...... P—N3!

Black prevents N—B5—a perfect example of the use of Pawn moves to cut down a Knight's mobility, as explained in the note to Black's 7th move. Now the prospects for the Knight look grim indeed.

26 B—K2 ......

Possibly with the idea of swinging his Queen to King Knight 3.

26 ...... P×P

Diagram 191

(Position after 26 ......
P×P)
*If now 27 BP×P, B—B1!
and Black threatens ......
P—B4 very strongly. If then
28 Q—KB3, B×Pch! wins
the Exchange for Black. And if
28 P—N4 White's King-side
is sadly weakened.*

Now the right way for White to recapture is 27 BP×P,

keeping his King Pawn at King 4 and thus preventing Black's King Pawn from advancing.

It is true that after 27 BP×P, B—QB1! Black would have the Queen-side majority of Pawns (an advantage for the endgame).

In addition, however, Black would also have a direct advantage for the middle game, as we can see in the caption to Diagram 191.

<blockquote>27   KP×P?   ......</blockquote>

No matter what the drawbacks of 27 BP×P might be, the move was unavoidable. For after the text move Black's King-side Pawns acquire fearsome agility.

<blockquote>27   ......   P—K5</blockquote>

Now Black begins to show his claws. The advance of the King Pawn threatens ...... B—B1 followed by ...... P—KN4 winning the Knight. (Again we see how the Knight's mobility is cut down by appropriate Pawn moves.)

<blockquote>28   P—N3   ......</blockquote>

White creates a retreat for his Knight at King Knight 2, but there is a heavy price to be paid for this Pawn move which weakens White's castled position.

<blockquote>28   ......   P—K6!</blockquote>

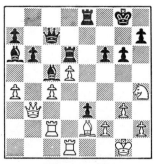

Diagram 192

(Position after 28 ......
P—K6!)
Black's further advance of his King Pawn puts White in a position of deadly danger. If now 29 P×P??, R×KP and no matter what White plays, the coming discovered check with Black's advanced Rook wins the White Queen!

29 P—B4   . . . . . .

We take it for granted that White must advance this Pawn.
But White also takes it for granted that he must advance the
Pawn *two squares*—and this is a mistake.

By playing 29 P—B3 White would achieve the same purpose of guarding against threats along the diagonal. At the
same time, he would protect the valuable King 4 square and
keep enemy pieces off that vital center square.

29 . . . . . .   B—B1!

Black realizes full well that sooner or later White's Knight
will have to leave its present square at the side of the board.
When that happens, Black will bring his Queen Bishop into
powerful play with . . . . . . B—B4.

Diagram 193

(Position after 29 . . . . . .
B—B1!)
*It is instructive to see how
efficiently Black switches all
his pieces to bear down on the
King-side.*

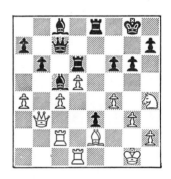

30 N—B3   . . . . . .

Ruefully White realizes that sooner or later this Knight
must attempt to get access to the center squares.

30 . . . . . .   B—B4

Attacking a White Rook. At last Black's Bishops are operating
with the sweeping power we expect of the Bishop-pair.

If White tries to intercept the attack on his Rook by playing
31 B—Q3??, Black wins outright by 31 . . . . . . P—K7 dis ch,
winning a Rook and promoting a new Queen.

Thus we see the enormous potential power of Black's passed

Pawn on King 6. Come what may, White is condemned to holding back this mighty Pawn.

    31 R—N2   ......

If only White can succeed in playing N—Q4 his Knight will at last be taking an active part in the game and he will be on the way to neutralizing the power of the Black Bishops.

    31 ......   R—K5!

Nothing doing, says Black. By centralizing this Rook (thanks to White's 29th move), Black prevents White from centralizing his Knight.

    32 K—N2   ......

White prudently removes his King from the dangerous diagonal. In this way he hopes to be able to move his Bishop from King 2.

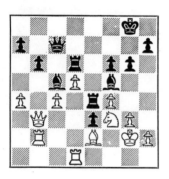

Diagram 194

(Position after 32 K—N2)
White is making a desperate effort to plug up the holes in the white squares on the King-side. It is these squares that Black will soon penetrate to achieve victory.

    32 ......   Q—B1!

Black's Queen is preparing to take part in the coming assault on White's King.

    33 N—N1   ......

White tries to plug the gaping holes in his King-side. The Knight move, for example, prevents ...... B—KR6ch.

    33 ......   P—KN4!

The tragedy of White's position is that he has too many weaknesses to be able to defend them all. Something has to give.

Diagram 195

(Position after 33 ......
P—KN4!)
*Step by step Black is making
further inroads on the
King-side.*

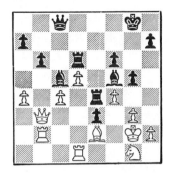

The purpose of Black's last move is to open up the King-side so that it will be easier for Black to get at the White King. On the most obvious level Black's threat is simply 34 ...... P×P; 35 P×P, R×KBP. This would further expose White's King and threaten ...... B—K5ch or ...... R—B7ch with devastating effect.

In the event of 34 B—B3 Black is prepared to sacrifice the Exchange, if need be, relying on his powerful Bishops to see him through: 34 B—B3, P×P!; 35 B×R, B×Bch; 36 N—B3 (if 36 K—B1, P—B6 is murderous), Q—N5; 37 R—KB1, P—B4!; 38 Q—Q1, R—N3!; 39 Q—K1, B—Q3! and White is helpless against the coming 40 ...... P×P; 41 P×P, B×NP etc.

Even 34 R—KB1 is not good enough: 34 R—KB1, P×P; 35 R×P, R×R; 36 P×R, R—Q2!; 37 Q—Q1, R—KN2ch; 38 K—R1, B—K5ch; 40 B—B3, P—K7! winning on the spot.

        34   P×P   ......

As we have seen in the previous note, White has nothing better.

        34   ......   P×P

As a result of the foregoing Pawn exchange, Black's Rook on Queen 3 can now swing over to the King-side. Move by move Black's Bishops take over more portentous power.

        35   R—KB1   ......

White tries to prop up his defenses by bringing his Rook

to the King-side. His great difficulty in conducting a satisfactory defense is that his Rook at Queen Knight 2 and his Queen at Queen Knight 3 contribute nothing to the defense.

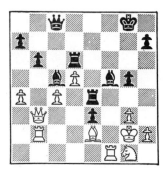

Diagram 196

(Position after 35 R—KB1)
*Black's coming ...... P—N5!
will reduce the Knight to
immobility.*

35 ...... P—N5!

Another characteristic Pawn move played to reduce the mobility of the Knight, which now has no moves at all!

36 B—Q3 ......

Not so much with the idea of winning the Exchange (which would be disastrous!) as to make room for N—K2—B4, which he hopes will bolster up his sagging King-side.

36 ...... R—KB3

Diagram 197

(Position after 36 ......
R—KB3)
*Black has calmly left his Rook
en prise on King 5, for
37 B × R?, B × Bch would be
immediately disastrous for
White.*

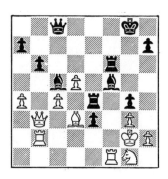

37 N—K2 ......

So that he can play 38 B × R, B × Bch; 39 K—N1.

37 ...... Q—B1!

Black keeps up the pressure relentlessly. If now 38 B×R??, B×Bch winning outright.

There are other points to this subtle and powerful Queen move. One is the coming ...... Q—R3, which introduces the final phase of Black's attack.

Another interesting aspect of the Queen move is that it provides a winning attack in the event of 38 N—B4. This move looks attractive because it seems to block the King Bishop file. Unfortunately for White, it allows the ferocious King Pawn to advance: 38 ...... P—K7!!; 39 R—K1, Q—R3; and wins, for example 40 R/N2×P, R×N; 41 P×R, Q—R6ch etc.

And after 38 N—B4, P—K7!!; 39 N×P, R×Nch!; 40 R×R, B—K5ch!! White is lost: 41 R×B, R—B7ch followed by checkmate, or 41 B×B, R×R and Black must win.

    38   R/N2—N1   ......

Diagram 198

(Position after 38 R/N2—N1)
*By protecting his King Rook
with his last move, White hopes
to be able to play B×R.*

    38   ......   Q—R3!

We must admire Black's artistry in finding ways to prevent B×R.

Thus if 39 B×R, B×Bch; 40 K—N1, Q—R6!; 41 N—B4, R×N! wins.

And if 39 N—B4, P—K7!! wins, for example 40 B×P, R×Bch; 41 N×R, B—K5ch etc.

Crushing Attack ■ 165

Of course if 39 R×B, R×R; 40 B×R, R—B7ch and Black mates next move.

        39 Q—B2   . . . . . .

Now it begins to look as if Black has overreached himself. White now doubly attacks Black's advanced Rook, which cannot retreat. How does Black escape from this dilemma?

        39 . . . . . .   Q—R6ch

The prelude to one of the most beautiful lines of play ever discovered on the chessboard.

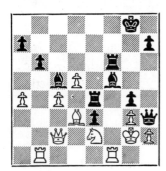

Diagram 199

(Position after 39 . . . . . . Q—R6ch)
White has to decide : which is the right King move for him to play?

If White plays 40 K—N1, he is once more on the same diagonal with Black's devilish King Bishop. There follows 40 . . . . . . R—R3 threatening mate. If then 41 N—B4 (or 40 N—B1 or 40 N—B3) to stop the mate, Black plays 41 . . . . . . P—K7 dis ch and wins at once!

        40   K—R1   . . . . . .

Offering Black the tempting possibility 40 . . . . . . R—R3?; 41 N—N1!, Q×NP when 42 Q—KN2! wins for White.

Instead, Black finds an exceedingly beautiful move.

        40 . . . . . .   R×P!!!

A move of really superb imaginative splendor. How many players could find this move and its dazzling sequel?

Since, as we shall see from the game continuation, 41 Q×R cannot save the game, it is tempting to speculate on other possibilities for White.

Diagram 200

(Position after 40 ......
R×P!!!)

The beauty of Black's last move is that White is left with no satisfactory way of capturing. If 41 B×R, B×Q wins; while the retreat Q—Q1??, R—R3! wins immediately for Black.

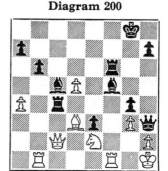

The great Capablanca suggested, for example, that White try 41 R×B?!, R×Q?; 42 R×R leading to a position in which Black's attack is dissipated and White has excellent practical chances.

However, on 41 R×B?! Black wins with 41 ...... R—R3!! threatening checkmate.

Now if White tries 42 N—N1 (to stop the mate), we get 42 ...... R×Q; 43 N×Q, R—Q7!; 44 N—B4, R/Q7×Pch; 45 K—N1, R—R8ch; 46 K—N2, R/R3—R7 mate.

And consider this possibility, starting from Diagram 200: 41 R×B?!, R—R3!!; 42 R—N5ch, K—B1; 43 R—B5ch, K—K2!; 44 P—Q6ch, K×P; 45 N—N1, R×Q; 46 N×Q, R—Q7!; 47 R×B, R×N!; 48 R—B3, R/Q7×Pch; 49 K—N1, R—R8ch; 50 K—N2, R/R6—R7 mate! (Even here the deadly King Pawn plays a useful role.)

You may find these variations heavy going, but they are worth playing over several times. Once you have mastered their intricacies, your admiration for Black's magnificent play will be considerably greater.

41 Q×R   ......

The only move—and very obvious, too. What's wrong with it? (If 41 ...... R—R3?; 42 P—Q6 dis ch!, B—K3; 43 Q× Bch!, R×Q; 44 B—B4, Q—R3; 45 N—B4 etc.).

Diagram 201

(Position after 41 . . . . . .
B×B!)
*To his horror White realizes
that if 42 Q×B, R—R3
forces mate at once. Black's
Bishops control the board.*

         41 . . . . . .   B×B!

Obvious—yet very powerful.

         42 R×R   . . . . . .

A last desperate try. White reconciles himself to the loss
of his Queen, as he perceives that he can win Black's Queen.

         42 . . . . . .   B×Q

         43 N—B4   . . . . . .

Trapping Black's Queen. But Black has the last word after
all.

         43 . . . . . .   P—K7!

The long-deferred triumph of Black's mighty passed Pawn.
If now 44 N×Q, B×Pch; 45 R—B3, B×R mate. As we have
seen in so many earlier positions, whenever the passed Pawn
can advance, the opening of the Black King Bishop's diagonal
spells disaster for White.

Diagram 202

(Position after 43 . . . . . .
P—K7!)
*Black's Queen is untouchable.
Meanwhile Black threatens
. . . . . . Q—B8ch.*

44	R—KN1	. . . . . .

White is pathetically helpless.

44	. . . . . .	Q—B8!
	Resigns	

Summary:

It is extremely instructive to review the course of this game. Once Black had the minute advantage of two Bishops against Bishop and Knight, he had a potential advantage.

Then, when Black played purposefully and White dawdled, the initial equilibrium was disturbed and Black's advantage became more and more marked.

Soon it was clear that White's game had no future. Yet it was not easy for Black to drive home his advantage. When his position had reached its most favorable state, he had to play forceful, imaginative chess.

And that is the way the crisis usually develops. The advantage previously obtained does not win of itself. *Gaining the advantage is not the same as victory; gaining the advantage merely provides the materials for achieving victory.*

LESSON 9: PSYCHOLOGY OF A POSITIONAL GAMBIT

A century ago and more, gambits were the most popular openings. The term "gambit" is used for openings in which one of the players gives away material in the hope of getting more than adequate compensation later on.

What kind of compensation? In the old days, the gambits were played to obtain a quick attack. In the King's Gambit (1 P—K4, P—K4; 2 P—KB4) White hoped to gain a quick attack along the King Bishop file. In the Danish Gambit (1 P—K4, P—K4; 2 P—Q4, P×P; 3 P—QB3 with the normal continuation 3 . . . . . . P×P; 4 B—QB4, P×P; 5 B×NP) White expected to score a brilliant victory through the powerful action of his Bishops.

These old-time gambits had these objectives:

1. Quick development.

2. Powerful Pawn center.

3. Rapid attack against the opponent's King.

From 1870 on, there was such an improvement in defensive play that these speculative openings came to be frowned on. The defender could capture material in the opening, dispose of the attack, and then win handily through his material advantage.

The result was that gambits were discredited. The masters played safe, conservative openings that often led to dreary, long-winded chess. But our game is one that necessarily flourishes on conflict, and eventually enterprising players evolved what was essentially a new kind of gambit—the "positional gambit."

In this type of opening, a player sacrifices material on a speculative basis—just as in the old gambits. But in the modern gambits he has no specific goal. His compensation for the sacrificed material lies in some positional advantage which may or may not be good enough to win.

All this sounds rather nebulous, and often enough it is. But to play such an opening—for either side—requires iron nerves, and a good deal of resourcefulness. On paper the defender may seem to have an easy game, but in the heat of the battle it is not always easy to find the right move. The defender becomes puzzled, then wary, and finally unsure of himself. Every move he examines seems to have some drawback. As the situation becomes more and more difficult, he may make a palpably wrong choice—and damage his position beyond redemption.

This is what happens in the game in this lesson. White has a perfectly safe position which offers good chances. Instead he courageously embarks on a purely speculative sacrifice of the Exchange. In return he has complete mastery of the black squares and a big lead in development.

Black is at a loss for a promising continuation. This is truly a situation in which "he who hesitates is lost." Soon Black finds himself enmeshed in difficulties which he cannot clear up. The stage is set for an incisive attack which enables White to win with astonishing rapidity. This is the typical course of a positional gambit.

KING'S INDIAN DEFENSE

WHITE	BLACK
1 P—Q4	. . . . . .

White plays this move in expectation of a Queen's Gambit—the opening we saw in the previous game. But instead of answering ...... P—Q4, Black selects a different course.

1 ......   N—KB3

Black chooses a waiting course. He can transpose into the Queen's Gambit Declined if he wishes, or he may choose a totally different course. By selecting the Knight move, Black preserves many options.

2 P—QB4   ......

Even now White is still unclear about the form that the opening will take.

2 ......   P—KN3

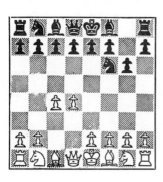

Diagram 203

(Position after 2 ...... P—KN3)
Black intends to fianchetto his King Bishop, which he expects to exert powerful pressure on the long diagonal.

3 P—KN3   ......

White follows suit; he will also fianchetto his King Bishop, with a view to controlling the long diagonal.

3 ......   B—N2

Black views White's Queen Pawn as a target for attack by his fianchettoed Bishop.

4 B—N2   ......

If Black wishes, he can now try to counteract the pressure of White's fianchettoed Bishop by playing 4 ...... P—B3 and if 5 N—QB3, P—Q4.

4 ......   P—Q4

Instead, Black decides on a very daring plan. He wants to

open up the center, even at the cost of losing time. The idea is to increase the scope of his fianchettoed Bishop. The whole plan involves risks for both players.

     5 P×P   . . . . . .

White is glad to capture, as he looks forward to building up a powerful center and gaining time by driving off Black's wandering Knight.

     5 . . . . . .   N×P

If White develops quietly by 6 N—KB3, Castles; 7 Castles, Black achieves equality by the flank thrust at White's center: 7 . . . . . . P—QB4!

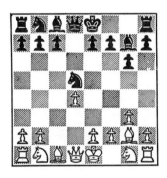

Diagram 204

(Position after 5 . . . . . . N×P)
Black is well prepared for White's coming P—K4. He anticipates that the resulting fracas in the center will yield him good counterchances.

     6 P—K4   . . . . . .

Black must make a radical choice between active and passive play. Thus, after 6 . . . . . . N—KB3 he blocks his fianchettoed Bishop and has no counterplay.

It is true that 6 . . . . . . N—N3 has the virtue of keeping the diagonal of Black's King Bishop open. But a Knight is generally badly placed at the Queen Knight 3 square because it has little effect on the center.

This maxim holds true here, for after 6 . . . . . . N—N3; 7 N—K2, Castles; 8 Castles, P—QB4; 9 P—Q5! Black's pieces are in a disquieting jumble on the Queen-side.

     6 . . . . . .   N—N5

On the face of it, 6 . . . . . . N—N5 looks like a mistake because of 7 Q—R4ch, N/N5—B3?; 8 P—Q5 winning a piece.

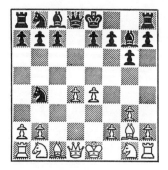

Diagram 205

(Position after 6 ......
N—N5)
*Black's last move is trappy:
if now 7 N—K2?, B×P!;
8 N×B, Q×N; 9 Q×Q,
N—B7ch and Black ends up a
Pawn ahead.*

Even after 7 Q—R4ch, N/N1—B3!; 8 P—Q5 it looks as
if Black must lose a piece. But this is not so, as he can simply
castle and answer 9 P×N with 9 ...... N—Q6ch. In that case,
White cannot move his King to the Queen file because of ......
N—B4 dis ch winning White's Queen. White must therefore
play 10 K—B1, allowing 10 ...... N×B in reply.

In addition, on 7 Q—R4ch, N/N1—B3!; 8 P—Q5 Black
has another good reply in 8 ...... P—QN4!; 9 Q×NP (on 9
Q—N3? Black wins with 9 ...... N—Q5!), N—B7ch; 10 K—
Q1, B—Q2! Now White finds that 11 K×N?? will not do
because of 11 ...... N—Q5ch, while 11 P×N?? fails because
of 11 ...... B×P dis ch.

       7   P—Q5   ......

White saves his Queen Pawn. Meanwhile Black's advanced
Knight is safe enough despite its dangerous-looking situation.

Above all, Black is gratified by the splendid diagonal of
his King Bishop. Note that the fianchettoed Bishop strikes all
the way down the diagonal, making it impossible for White
to develop his Queen Bishop.

       7   ......   P—QB3!

A flank thrust at the center. If Black can succeed in forcing
the removal of White's Queen Pawn, he will have won the
battle of the opening.

In the event of 8 P—QR3 Black intends 8 ...... Q—R4!

with a fine game. He does not fear 9 B—Q2? in reply, for then he has 9 ...... N—Q6ch; 10 K—K2, Q—R3!

    8   N—K2   ......

White would like to castle quickly in order to eliminate all counterthreats against his King.

However, Black can keep the pot boiling with 8 ...... P×P; 9 P×P, B—B4 (threatens ...... N—B7ch); 10 Q—R4ch, N/N1—B3! (for if 11 P×N??, N—B7ch; 12 K—B1, Q—Q8 mate!); 11 QN—B3 and now Black has tremendous counterplay with 11 ...... B—B7! or 11 ...... P—QN4!

    8   ......   Castles

A good move on principle; but by relaxing for a moment, Black gives White a chance to catch his breath.

    9   Castles   ......

A plausible line here is 9 ...... P×P; 10 P×P, B—B4; 11 QN—B3, N—B7?; 12 P—KN4!, N×R; 13 P×B. White will capture Black's daring Knight and be ahead in material.

    9   ......   P—K3!?

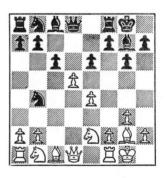

Diagram 206

(Position after 9 ......
P—K3!?)
Black hopes to clear the center.
After 10 P×BP, QN×P or
10 P×KP, B×KP he would
have a splendid position.

It is true that White can retain some positional advantage with 10 P—QR3, N/N5—R3; 11 QN—B3, KP×P; 12 P×P, P×P; 13 N×P, thanks to the commanding centralized position of his Queen Knight.

But it seems a pity to allow Black's fianchettoed Bishop to keep the mighty diagonal. So, after a good deal of soul-searching, White decides on a very complicated and daring line of play.

10   B—Q2!!?   . . . . . .

White offers the Exchange and a Pawn for a highly speculative venture.

Black can hardly decline, for example 10 . . . . . . N—Q6; 11 B—QB3!, N×NP; 12 Q—N3, B×B (forced); 13 QN×B, N—Q6; 14 KR—Q1 with a terrific position. Black seems to have nothing better than 14 . . . . . . N—B4, but after 15 Q—R3! White has an enormous lead in development and powerful pressure. Note that 15 . . . . . . Q—N3? will not do because of 16 QR—N1; likewise 15 . . . . . . Q—K2? fails because of 16 P—Q6.

So Black must play 15 . . . . . . N/B4—Q2, leaving White with a tremendous position in return for the sacrificed Pawn after 16 P×KP, P×P; 17 P—K5! etc.

10   . . . . . .   B×P

Black has achieved the utmost with his fianchettoed Bishop —yet his troubles are only starting.

11   B×N   . . . . . .

What compensation will White have for his sacrifice?

11   . . . . . .   B×R

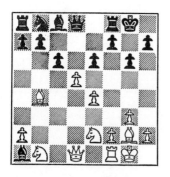

Diagram 207

(Position after 11 . . . . . .
B×R)
White can now regain the Exchange with 12 B×R, but in that case he will still remain without any compensation for the Pawn minus.

12   QN—B3!   . . . . . .

The right idea. White will force Black's King Bishop to

disappear while he retains his own black-square Bishop. In view of the holes in Black's King-side, Black will be weak on the black squares. White's black-square Bishop will exert enormous pressure precisely because his opposite number will be gone from the board.

White will also be ahead in development. But this is a point which we can appraise more clearly a little later.

| 12 | ...... | B×N |

The exchange is unavoidable, for after 12 ...... B—N7 White gains more time for development with 13 Q—N3.

| 13 | N×B | ...... |

White has three pieces in active play, while Black has none. His Queen-side pieces are still all on their original squares. White's problem is this: can he organize decisive action on the black squares before Black completes his development?

The fate of the game will depend on the answer to this question. Both players are racing against time.

| 13 | ...... | R—K1 |

Another way was 13 ...... N—R3, gaining time for development. Black could philosophically permit 14 B×R, on the theory that he would still be a Pawn ahead and that most of the steam would go out of White's attacking chances once he parts with the black-square Bishop.

However, the drawback to 13 ...... N—R3 is that it develops the Knight *away from the center*. White simply retreats 14 B—QR3 and Black does not seem to have made much progress, since he hasn't solved the problems of protecting the black squares and fighting for control of the center.

Thinking along these lines gives Black a feeling of discouragement and uncertainty. This is precisely the result that White wants to achieve.

Black's psychological difficulty in this type of position is that he cannot find a line of play that is wholly satisfying. In playing 13 ...... R—K1, for example, Black hopes to block

the center and close the black-square long diagonal with ......
P—K4. Yet it is precisely because of this would-be blocking
move that White is later able to play 18 P—B4!, opening the
diagonal for his Bishop and the King Bishop file for his Rook.

The inconclusiveness of Black's plans naturally has a very
disturbing effect. This is bound to rob him of the incisive
mood that he needs in order to play resourcefully.

14   Q—B1!   ......

A menacing move which artfully underlines Black's uncertainty. The text is a broad hint that White intends to play
Q—R6, with powerful pressure on Black's woefully weak
black squares.

Black can prevent this with 14 ...... K—N2, but then his
development is still in arrears and there is always the possibility
that White's Queen Bishop will get back on the long diagonal
with threats against Black's King.

Perhaps Black should make a violent break for freedom
with 14 ...... P—QR4; 15 B—QR3, P—QN4 (threatening to
win a piece with ...... P—N5); 16 B—N2, P—N5; 17 N—R4,
BP×P. Now Black has even won a second Pawn.

However the sudden opening up of the position favors
White, whose actively posted pieces develop great effectiveness,
for example: 18 Q—R6 (threatens mate!), P—B3; 19 P×P,
P×P; 20 R—Q1, B—K3; 21 N—B5, B—B2; 22 N—K4!,
N—Q2; 23 N—Q6!, R—K2; 24 N×B, R×N; 25 B×QP
with terrific pressure on Black's game.

So we see that the outlook for Black's game is very dis-
couraging. Whichever way Black plays, he runs into trouble.

14   ......   P—K4

Black hopes that he can at least block off White's pressure
on the long diagonal leading to his King Knight 2 square.

15   B—QR3   ......

An ominous preparation for further action on the long
diagonal.

Note, by the way, that 15 P—B4? (in order to open the diagonal and the King Bishop file) is a huge blunder at this point because the double attack 15 . . . . . . Q—N3ch wins a piece.

Diagram 208

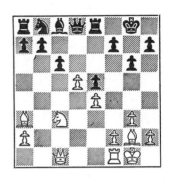

(Position after 15 B—QR3)
Black has still failed to make any progress toward developing his minor pieces. Perhaps 15 . . . . . . Q—R4 might be suitable, as it ties White's Queen down to its present square for a while.

Again a puzzling situation for Black. He is afraid to play 15 . . . . . . Q—R4 because then his Queen would be too far away from the King-side. Again we see that no matter how he proceeds, he is pursued by nagging doubts.

$$15 \quad \ldots\ldots \qquad\qquad P \times P$$

Another two-edged move. Black reasons this way: if White recaptures with 16 P×P, Black can reply 16 . . . . . . B—B4, finally getting in some good development. On the other hand, if White recaptures with 16 N×P, Black can at last play 16 . . . . . . N—B3, giving his Knight a chance to bear on important center squares.

True, White is able to centralize his Knight powerfully on the Queen 5 square, but Black figures on playing . . . . . . B—K3 in a move or two, getting rid of the powerful Knight if the situation calls for that.

All very plausibly reasoned, but Black forgets several things. In the first place, White is considerably ahead in development. *In such cases, any opening up of the position favors the player with the superior development, as he can attack more efficiently than his opponent can defend.*

After all, if White attacks with three very well posted pieces and Black "defends" with his lone King, what result can we expect but a resounding victory for White? And if the lines are opened so that White's attacking forces have vastly increased scope, White's attack will obviously be more powerful than ever.

The other point that Black has to reckon with is that White has the two Bishops. As we know from the previous game, the Bishop-pair can unleash tremendous power in an open position. So far White's King Bishop has been a mere bystander, but once the position opens up, this piece will come into strong play.

16   N×P   ......

Let's see some possibilities: if 16 ...... K—N2 (still no development!); 17 N—B7, N—R3; 18 N×QR, B—K3; 19 P—B4!, Q×N; 20 B—N2! with a winning attack on the long diagonal.

Or 16 ...... B—K3; 17 P—B4!, B×N; 18 P×B, P—K5; 19 P—B5! with a winning attack.

16   ......   N—B3

Black hopes to play 17 ...... B—K3, getting rid of the powerful Knight.

17   Q—R6!

Diagram 209

(Position after 17 Q—R6!)
White's attack has now taken on menacing proportions.

White's overwhelming control of the black squares promises to yield results, as Black cannot get rid of the splendidly centralized·Knight at this stage.

Thus, if 17 ...... B—K3 White has 18 B—K7! Then if 18 ...... R×B (or 18 ...... N×B); 19 N—B6ch, K—R1; 20 Q×RP mate.

Or if 17 ...... B—K3; 18 B—K7!, Q—B1; 19 B—B6 or N—B6ch followed by mate. (Note White's exclusive control of the black squares.)

Finally, if 17 ...... B—K3; 18 B—K7!, Q×B; 19 N×Qch, R×N Black has approximate material equality, but after 20 P—B4! White has a winning attack.

17 ......   P—B3

This at least stops 18 B—K7, for after 18 ...... R×B; 19 N×Pch, Black's King can escape to King Bishop 2.

18 P—B4!   ......

Now White brings his Rook into the game by posing new threats on the King Bishop file. White's immediate threat is obvious but nonetheless powerful; 19 P×P followed by a murderous Knight check at King Bishop 6.

Diagram 210

(Position after 18 P—B4!)
Black has great difficulty defending himself against the concentrated attack of White's forces.

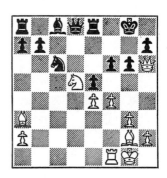

Note that it's too late to play 18 ...... B—K3, for then comes 19 P×P!, B×N; 20 P×P! threatening Q—N7 mate. If then 20 ...... Q—Q2; 21 P×B with the double threat of 22

P×N and 22 P—B7ch. (Here we see how White's Rook operates on the newly opened King Bishop file.)

If Black tries 18 ...... P×P then we get 19 R×P (still operating on the open file), R—K3; 20 B—R3! (now White's Bishops are in their element), R—Q3 (if 20 ...... P—B4; 21 R—R4, Q—Q2; 22 Q—B8 mate or 22 ...... R—K2; 23 N×Rch and wins); 21 B×R, Q×B; 22 N×Pch and wins.

| 18 ...... | P—B4 |

Black is striving desperately to neutralize the power of White's infiltration, but his task is very difficult.

| 19 BP×P | ...... |

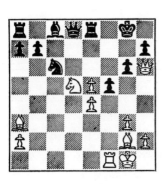

Diagram 211

(Position after 19 BP×P)
The momentum of White's attack is increasing move by move.

Simple and strong. White's immediate threat is N—B6ch, so Black must play ...... R×P or ...... N×P.

If Black tries 19 ...... N×P, then 20 P×P, B×P; 21 P—R3! and Black is helpless against the coming 22 P—N4.

So Black decides to try 19 ...... R×P, although this allows White's Rook to come into powerful action on another open file.

Note, by the way, that the influence of White's King Bishop is becoming more and more marked as the game opens up.

| 19 ...... | R×P |
| 20 R—Q1 | ...... |

Taking a new file with the threat of 21 N—K7ch winning Black's Queen.

20 ......   B—Q2

Parrying the threat. At last Black has his minor pieces in play. This gives him some hope of successful resistance.

21   B—N2   ......

This does not really threaten B×R, which would only diminish the pressure on Black's game.

White's real threat is 22 N—B6ch!, Q×N; 23 R×B, N—K2; 24 R×P and White is sure of recovering the Exchange and meanwhile maintains the pressure.

21 ......   B—K3

Desperately hoping to get rid of the terrible Knight.

22   P×P!   ......

Nicely played. The beautiful point is that Black cannot play 22 ...... R×N? because of 23 Q—N7 mate. (Again and again the theme of White's mastery of the black squares recurs in this game.)

And if 22 ...... B×N; 23 B×Bch, K—R1 (Black cannot capture the Bishop!); 24 P×P and wins. For example 24 ...... Q—K2; 25 B—B7 forcing mate. Once more White's stranglehold on the black squares is the theme of victory. And again we see the enormous power of White's Bishops.

Black's formal advantage in material (represented by his useless Queen Rook) is of no use to him in this critical situation. His only chance is to be able to return the Exchange at a suitable moment.

22 ......   B×P

If 22 ...... P×P; 23 N—B6ch wins for White. (Again action on the black squares is decisive!)

23   P—KR3!   ......

Black's position is apparently a picture of helplessness. White's centralized Knight, ably abetted by White's crisscross Bishops, controls the board.

Yet, after all that Black has been through, he can squirm out of the attack if he plays 23 ...... Q—KB1!

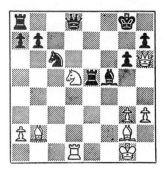

Diagram 212

(Position after 23 P—KR3!)
*White's last threatens 24 P—
N4 followed (after
preparation) by P—N5 and
N—B6ch and wins.*

In that event, 24 Q—B4, QR—K1!; 25 P—N4 will not
do because of 25 . . . . . . R×N!; 26 B×Rch, B—K3 and White
has nothing to show for his Pawn minus.

So, after 23 . . . . . . Q—KB1! White must play 24 Q×Qch. If
then 24 . . . . . . R×Q; 25 B×R, N×B; 26 N—K7ch, K—B2;
27 N×B, P×N; 28 B×P with material equality and a micro-
scopic advantage for White because of his long-range Bishop.
However, the ending would probably be a draw.

Or 23 . . . . . . Q—KB1!; 24 Q×Qch; K×Q; 25 B×R, N×B;
26 P—N4!, B—Q2; 27 N—B6 and White recovers the Pawn
with an even ending.

| 23 | . . . . . . | B—K3? |

This loses. Black has had too much punishment, and is now
too disheartened and too confused to find the best move.
Consequently he loses very quickly.

This is a typical occurrence in a game which has started
with a positional gambit. Ultimately, the strain proves too
much for the defender.

| 24 | B×R | N×B |
| 25 | Q—K3! | . . . . . . |

Pinning Black's Knight. Black finds himself without a good
defense.

Thus, if 25 . . . . . . Q—Q3; 26 N—B6ch wins Black's Queen.

And if 25 . . . . . . B×N; 26 R×B (not 26 Q×N, Q—N3ch!),
N—Q2; 27 Q—Q4 winning the pinned Knight. Another way
is 26 B×Bch, N—B2; 27 B×Nch winning Black's Queen.

Diagram 213

(Position after 24 . . . . . .
N×B)
*White can now set up a
crippling pin.*

| 25 | . . . . . . | Q—N1 |
| 26 | R—K1! | Resigns |

He has no defense, for if 26 . . . . . . B×N; 27 B×Bch N—
B2; 28 R—KB1 and the new pin wins for White.

Summary:

This game is a fine illustration of the positional gambit.
When the attacker offers such a gambit, he looks forward to
obtaining a position that will be too complicated for the
defender to handle.

After White's surprising sacrifice of the Exchange, he had so
much pressure on the black squares and such a great lead in
development that Black's defensive task was exceedingly
difficult.

Yet he managed to defend himself with great patience up
to a point. What he forgot was that in positions of this type
the defender generally has one sovereign remedy: *to return
the extra material in order to draw off the attack.* This valuable tactic is illustrated in the note to White's 23rd move—the
crucial point of the game.

Had Black resorted to this tactic, he would have saved the
game. Missing the point, he was soon overwhelmed by the
onrush of White's attack.

You are now ready to go on to the endgame, the most
difficult and fascinating part of the game.

LESSON 10:

WHAT THE ENDGAME

IS ALL ABOUT

On the face of it, the endgame stage of a game of chess is the easiest part of the game. Many exchanges have taken place; only the Kings, some Pawns and a few pieces are left.

And yet the very simplicity of the situation creates problems. Some players feel that with the removal of the Queens most of the fun has gone out of the game. Others know that they are supposed to end the game—but don't know how. Where can we find a guiding principle?

The endgame is just that: *the end of the game*. This is the stage in which all loose ends are tied up, all accounts settled. Let us assume that one of the players is ahead in material; then he ought to win in the simplified endgame stage, for at this point the weaker side can no longer create complications or diversions.

Clearly, then, our endgame goal must be checkmate. The most basic forms of checkmate are those which can be achieved with a minimum number of forces.

The easiest of these checkmates is the one with King and Queen against lone King. This brings us to the second of the two vital aspects of endgame play.

We know that if we have a King and Queen against a lone King we can force checkmate. But what many players do not realize is that a King and Pawn have practically the same power against a hostile King. How so?

A player who is a Pawn ahead should be able to promote this Pawn to a Queen. He can then achieve checkmate. If he has King and Pawn against King, this should be relatively simple to achieve.

If a player has, say, five Pawns against four of his opponent's, he should still be able to win in similar fashion, if he has a passed Pawn. (A passed Pawn is one which is not opposed by hostile Pawns on an adjoining file. A passed Pawn is therefore a favored candidate for queening, and the further it advances the more dangerous it becomes.)

Suppose a player is a Pawn ahead and doesn't have a passed Pawn. In that case he advances his Pawns until they come in contact with the enemy's Pawns, and sooner or later a passed Pawn must be crystallized from this contact.

These King and Pawn endings will be dealt with first. Before you go on, however, review the basic checkmates in Lesson 4.

King and Pawn Endings

It is in this type of ending that we see posed in the most fundamental way the struggle to promote a Pawn to Queen. If the Pawn can be queened, then we know that checkmate cannot be far off. That is why, in practical play, a player will generally resign when his opponent promotes a Pawn successfully. Resignation may even come earlier, in fact, when it is clear that checkmate cannot be avoided.

Diagrams 214 through 218 may be considered the basic examples of this type of ending. The more complex endings of Kings and Pawns will often reduce to these models—or else the play may revolve around the struggle to reach one of these positions.

As we shall see, these endings are often won or drawn on the

King and Pawn Endings ■ 187

basis of having the Opposition, a device which enables a player to force the opponent's King out of the way. The Kings are said to be in Opposition when they are placed on the same line—generally a file—and there is an odd number of squares between them. If a player has to move his King, his opponent has the Opposition. Because of the importance of this theme, it is essential to study the workings of the Opposition in Diagrams 214 and 215 before going on to other endings.

Diagram 214

This is a basic ending which illustrates the importance of the Opposition.

Diagram 215

Another basic ending. If it is Black's move, White has the Opposition and wins quickly.

In the position of Diagram 214, if it is Black's move, White has the Opposition and wins:

WHITE	BLACK
1	K—Q1
2 P—Q7	K—K2
3 K—B7 and wins	

White queens his Pawn.

If it is White's move, Black has the Opposition and draws:

1 P—Q7ch	K—Q1
2 K—Q6	Drawn

Black is stalemated. Note that 1 K—N6, K—Q2; 2 K—B5, K—Q1!; 3 K—B6, K—B1 still draws for Black, as he maintains the Opposition.

In the position of Diagram 215:

	WHITE	BLACK
1	......	K—Q1

Or 1 ...... K—B1; 2 K—Q7 and wins.

	WHITE	BLACK
2	K—B7	K—Q2
3	P—K6ch	K—Q1
4	P—K7ch and wins	

If it is White's move, Black has the Opposition but White can take it away from him:

	WHITE	BLACK
1	K—Q6	......

1 K—B6 also wins.

	WHITE	BLACK
1	......	K—Q1
2	P—K6!	......

The spare move with the Pawn gives White the Opposition. (Note the difference from Diagram 214.)

	WHITE	BLACK
2	......	K—K1
3	P—K7	K—B2
4	K—Q7 and wins	

Again the Pawn must queen.

Diagram 216

The third basic King and Pawn ending. White retains the Opposition no matter who moves first, thanks to the spare moves of his Pawn. If Black moves first, White wins.

	WHITE	BLACK
1	......	K—K2
2	K—B6	K—Q1
3	K—Q6	K—B1
4	P—Q4	K—Q1
5	P—Q5 and wins	

If 5 ...... K—K1; 6 K—B7 etc. as in the previous examples. Or 5 ...... K—B1; 6 K—K7 etc. In either case White controls the queening square.

If White moves first, he wins in similar fashion:

1	P—Q4!	K—K2
2	K—B6	K—Q1
3	K—Q6	K—K1
4	K—B7	K—K2
5	P—Q5	K—K1
6	P—Q6	K—B1
7	P—Q7 and wins	

Diagram 217

White to move.
Black's King is too far away from the critical sector to be able to stop White's distant passed Pawn.

	WHITE	BLACK
1	P—R4!	K—N3
2	P—R5	K—B2
3	P—R6	K—K2
4	P—R7	K—Q2
5	P—R8/Q and wins	

Diagram 218

This ending—with a Rook Pawn—is always drawn regardless of who moves first. Black's King can never be dislodged from the corner, and the steady advance of the Pawn is bound to produce stalemate.

In the position of Diagram 218:

	WHITE	BLACK
1	P—R5	K—N1
2	K—N6	K—R1
3	P—R6	K—N1
4	P—R7ch	K—R1
5	K—R6	Drawn

Black is stalemated.

Diagram 219

White to move.
*Although White can win
Black's Pawn, the ending is a
draw as Black can force the
standard drawing position.*

	WHITE	BLACK
1	K—N5	K—K3
2	K—B5	K—K2
3	K—Q5	K—B3
4	K—Q6	K—B2
5	K×P	K—K2

Black has the Opposition and cannot be driven out of it.

6	K—Q5	K—Q2
7	P—K5	K—K2
8	P—K6	K—K1!
9	K—Q6	K—Q1

Drawn. White can make no headway, for example 10 P—
K7ch, K—K1; 11 K—K6 with stalemate.

Diagram 220

White to move.
*With two Pawns ahead, White
wins effortlessly. Note that
connected passed Pawns are
capable of self-protection
without the aid of their King.*

	WHITE	BLACK
1	P—N6	K—B3

If 1 ...... K×P; 2 P—N7 wins.

	WHITE	BLACK
2	K—B4	K—K2
3	K—K5	K—B1
4	P—B6	K—N1
5	P—B7ch	K—B1
6	K—K6	K—N2
7	K—K7 and wins	

White continues with 8 P—B8/Q.

Diagram 221

White to move.
*Despite White's material
advantage the win is not easy.
If 1 K—B5, K—R1;
2 K—B6?? he stalemates
Black. The right way is:*

	WHITE	BLACK
1	P—R8/Qch!	K×Q

Now White wins by taking the Opposition on the sixth rank.

	WHITE	BLACK
2	K—R6	......

2 K—B6 also wins.

	WHITE	BLACK
2	......	K—N1

3	P—N7	K—B2
4	K—R7 and wins	

White queens his Pawn.

Diagram 222

White to move.
This ending illustrates the value of a distant passed Pawn; it also reveals the power of connected passed Pawns.

	WHITE	BLACK
1	P—R4!	K—B4

Sooner or later Black's King must be on hand to prevent the Rook Pawn from queening.

2	K—K4	K—N5

If now 3 K×P?, K×P; 4 K—Q4, K—N6 and Black draws.

3	P—N3!	K—R4

After 3 . . . . . . K×P; 4 P—R5 the White Pawn must queen.

4	K×P	K—N5
5	K—Q4	K—R4
6	K—B5	K—R3
7	P—N4 and wins	

Diagram 223

White to move.
White's outside passed Pawn wins for him, as Black has no counterchances on the other wing, where one White Pawn paralyzes two Black Pawns.

	WHITE	BLACK
1	P—R5	K—B3

King and Pawn Endings ■ 193

2	K—K5	K—N4
3	K—B6	K×P
4	K×NP	K—N3
5	K×P	K—B3
6	K—N6	K—Q2
7	P—B5	K—K1
8	K—N7 and wins	

The Pawn queens.

Diagram 224

Black to move.
Black's King is poised for invasion. As soon as White's Pawn moves give out, his King must allow the decisive advance of Black's King.

	WHITE	BLACK
1	......	P—R4!
2	K—B2	K—N5
3	K—N2	P—B4
	Resigns	

For if 4 K—B2, K—R6; 5 K—B3, K—R7; 6 K—B2, P—N3; 7 K—B3, K—N8; 8 K—K3, K—N7 and White can no longer defend his Pawns.

Thus we complete our study of King and Pawn endings. We can now pass to more complex endings in which there are additional pieces on the board. Again and again we shall find, however, that the possibility of reduction to a decisive King and Pawn ending plays an overriding role in the thinking of both players. Thus King and Pawn endings are not only important in themselves—they are also important as a model and a goal for more elaborate endings which at any moment may be resolved into a "simpler" form.

LESSON 11:

WINNING WHEN A
PIECE AHEAD

We continue with the basic idea that our supreme goal is checkmate. It follows, then, that gaining a material advantage contributes to the attainment of this goal. For a substantial advantage in material will give us a power over the enemy that will probably enable us to force checkmate, or to win more material with the same end in view. And of course having a material advantage will make it that much easier to enforce the promotion of a Pawn.

But in order to be able to obtain a material advantage and to be able to put it to use, we need to know the relative values of the chessmen and this is a good time to review their values as shown in Lesson 2.

The Queen is of course by far the strongest piece.

The Rook is the next strongest, definitely more powerful than a Bishop or Knight.

The Bishop and Knight are of equal value.

The Pawn is the weakest unit, but of course its promotion power has to be kept in mind. By successful promotion, it is converted from the weakest unit into the strongest.

The advantage of a piece ahead (say a Bishop or Knight) is considerable in the middle game. It must infallibly lead to checkmate or to further material gain.

In the endgame the advantage of a piece is above all instrumental in making it possible for a Pawn to queen. There are however occasional exceptions which it is useful to know.

Diagram 225

White to move.
White has an easy win, as he picks off both Black Pawns and then queens his own Pawn.

	WHITE	BLACK
1	K—N4	K—K3
2	K×P	K—B3
3	K×P and wins	

White wins easily by advancing his Pawn to the queening square.

Diagram 226

White to move.
Here the queening square is of the same color as those on which the Bishop moves. The win is quite simple.

	WHITE	BLACK
1	B—Q5ch	K—N1
2	P—R7ch	K—B1
3	P—R8/Qch and wins	

Diagram 227

White to move.
Here the queening square is "of the wrong color." White only draws, as the Black King cannot be budged out of the corner.

WHITE	BLACK
1 B—Q4	. . . . . .

Both 1 P—R7 and 1 B—K5 stalemate Black.

1	K—N1
2 B—K5ch	. . . . . .

Or 2 P—R7ch, K—R1 and stalemate ensues—unless White's King retreats.

2	K—R1
3 B—Q4	. . . . . .

Otherwise Black is stalemated.

3	K—N1

Drawn. Obviously White can make no headway.

Diagram 228

White to move.
The widely separated passed Pawns are too much for the Bishop, unassisted by his King.

WHITE	BLACK
1 P—B7	. . . . . .

Or 1 P—N7 etc.

1	K—B4

A Piece Ahead ■ 197

2	P—N7	K—K3
3	P—B8/Q	. . . . . .

Likewise 3 P—N8/Q wins.

3	. . . . . .	B×Q
4	P—N8/Q and wins	

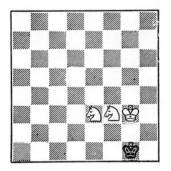

Diagram 229

Black to move.
It is well known, but perhaps not well understood, that two Knights cannot force checkmate. Consider the situation that arises after Black plays 1 . . . . . . K—R8.

After 1 . . . . . . K—R8 Black is in a stalemate position. This gives White no time for 2 N—N4 or 2 N—Q1 (with a view to 3 N—B2 mate). On the other hand, if White plays 2 N—K1 (or some other move of this Knight) he no longer has a mate threat.

Diagram 230

White to move.
A remarkable position; despite his material advantage White cannot win, as he has advanced his Pawn thoughtlessly and created a stalemate resource for Black.

	WHITE	BLACK
1	K—N5	K—R1
2	K—N6	Drawn

Other White moves are no better, as Black's King keeps moving back and forth between Queen Knight 2 and Queen Rook 1.

Diagram 231

White to move.

Here White has prudently held back his Rook Pawn and has an easy win.

	WHITE	BLACK
1	N—B5ch	K—R2
2	K—B6	......

White gains access to Queen Knight 6 for his King.

2	......	K—N1
3	K—N6	K—R1

Now White drives away the Black King from the corner.

4	N—K6!	K—N1
5	N—B7	K—B1
6	P—R6	K—N1
7	P—R7ch and wins	

The Pawn queens next move.

Diagram 232

White to move.

The strange paradox of this position is that Black loses because he has a Pawn left. Without the Pawn the position is of course a draw.

	WHITE	BLACK
1	N—B6!	......

And not 1 N—N3?? stalemating Black.

1	......	K—R8

2 N—K4!   K—R7

Or 2 ......P—R7; 3 N—N3 mate.

         3 N—Q2!   K—R8

         4 N—B1!   P—R7

         5 N—N3 mate

An attractive winning method.

Diagram 233

White to move.

This is the worst possible kind of situation for the Knight.

WHITE	BLACK
1 K—B6	N—R1
2 K—N7 and wins	

White wins the Knight and then queens his Pawn.

If Black's King were favorably placed—say at King 4 or King 2—he could now draw by 2 ...... K—Q3 (or some similar move); 3 K×N, K—B2 stalemating White.

Diagram 234

Black to move.

Compare this diagram with Diagram 229. Here White forces checkmate because the presence of the Pawn deprives Black of stalemate possibilities.

WHITE	BLACK
1	K—R8
2 N—Q1	......

But not 2 N—N4?? and Black is stalemated.

	2	......	P—N5
	3	N—B2 mate	

Diagram 235

White to move.
*With the Pawn off the board,
White draws. With the Pawn
on, White forces checkmate.*

	WHITE	BLACK
1	N—B2	K—R4

Black stays away from the corner as long as he can.

2	N/B2—N4	K—R5
3	K—N6	K—N6
4	K—N5	K—N7

Black's King is being steadily forced into the fatal corner.

5	K—B4	K—R8
6	K—B3	K—N8
7	K—N3	K—R8
8	N—B3	P—R7

The move that prevents stalemate.

	9	N—B2 mate	

Diagram 236

White to move.
*With two Pawns already far
advanced and with Black's last
Pawn marked for early
confiscation, White easily beats
down Black's defense. The
Knight is helpless here.*

	WHITE	BLACK
1	K—B4	N—Q7
2	K—K5	N—B6ch
3	K×P	N—R5

As White must part with at least one Pawn, he gives up his Rook Pawn and retains the Knight Pawn.

4	P—R8/Qch	K×Q
5	K—B7	N—B4

Forced.

6	P—K4	N—R3ch
7	K—B8	N—B4

Again the only move. Naturally White does not oblige by capturing the Knight and stalemating Black.

8	P—K5!	N—N2
9	K—B7	N—B4
10	P—K6	N—R3ch
11	K—B8	N—N1
12	P—B4	N—B3
13	K—B7	Resigns

If 13 ...... N—N1; 14 P—K7 wins easily.

Diagram 237

White to move.
While a Rook is often helpless against far advanced passed Pawns, split Pawns are usually an easy prey for the Rook. This position is an exception.

	WHITE	BLACK
1	K—B4	R—KB2

Black must go after the Pawns at once, else White's King gets too close. 1 ...... R—KR2 is no better than the text, for then 2 K—Q5, R×P; 3 K—K6 draws.

2	P—R7!	R×RP
3	K—Q5	Drawn

For 4 K—K6 saves the day.

Diagram 238

White to move.
White establishes the win at once by creating a barrier the Black King cannot cross. This gives White's King time to play an effective role.

WHITE	BLACK
1 R—R5!	P—N4
2 K—Q7	P—N5

Equally hopeless is 2 ...... K—N3; 3 K—K6, K—R4; 4 K—B5 and the Pawn is doomed.

3 K—Q6	K—N3

Or 3 ...... P—N6; 4 R—R3 winning the Pawn.

4 R—K5!	K—B3
5 K—Q5 and wins	

If 5 ...... P—N6; 6 R—K3 wins.

If 5 ...... K—N3; 6 K—Q4 and White's King can go after the Pawn.

LESSON 12:
ENDGAMES WITH BISHOPS
AND KNIGHTS

Bishop and Pawn Endings

Simple as many of these endings are, there is an art to winning them. Generally they involve the victorious advance of a passed Pawn to the queening square in positions where that advance looks deceptively easy.

A knowing player has many resources that enable him to fight for, and often secure, the draw. This lends a special intensity to the struggle, as does the fact that the defensive Bishop can often function at a considerable distance.

Endings with Bishops that move on opposite colors are particularly tricky. Here the Pawn position is everything, and,

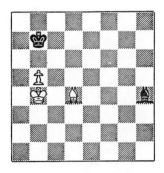

Diagram 239

A perfect position for the materially weaker side. Black's unassailable King can never be driven away from its blockading position. A clear draw.

though these endings are reputed to end in a draw most of the time, there are many—often unsuspected—winning possibilities in them.

Diagram 240

White to move.
Despite the effective position of Black's pieces, White can force the queening of his Pawn by a series of precise maneuvers.

	WHITE	BLACK
1	B—R4!	K—N3

Other moves lose even more rapidly, for example 1 ...... B—B5; 2 B—B2, B—R7; 3 B—R7, B—B5; 4 B—N8, B—K6; 5 B—N3, B—R2; 6 B—B2! and wins. Black tries to stave off this variation by bringing his King to Queen Rook 3.

2	B—B2ch	K—R3
3	B—B5!	......

To force Black's Bishop off his present square.

3	......	B—N6
4	B—K7	K—N3

Back again, as White was threatening to win with B—Q8—B7.

5	B—Q8ch	K—B3
6	B—R4!	......

The winning tempo, made possible at move 3.

6	......	B—Q3
7	B—B2	B—R7
8	B—R7	B—Q3
9	B—N8	B—B4
10	B—R2	B—R2
11	B—N1 and wins	

Black's Bishop has become useless.

Diagram 241

White to move.
*Two passed Pawns, when far
apart, win easily. But even
when there is only one file
between them they still win,
despite the narrow front on
which the defense is
concentrated.*

	WHITE	BLACK
1	P—B4ch	K—Q3
2	P—B5	K—K4
3	P—Q4ch	K—B3
4	K—B4	B—N6
5	B—B6	B—B7

It is curious that White can make further progress without
getting his King to King 5.

6	B—Q7	B—N6
7	K—K4	B—B5

If 7 . . . . . . B—B7ch; 8 K—Q5 wins.

8	P—Q5	B—N6
9	B—K6!	B—B5
10	K—Q4	B—K7

Or 10 . . . . . . B—R7; 11 K—B5 and wins.

11	P—Q6	B—N4
12	P—Q7!	K—K2
13	P—B6ch	K—Q1
14	P—B7	K—K2
15	P—B8/Qch	K×Q
16	P—Q8/Qch and wins	

Diagram 242

Black to move.

Two connected passed Pawns on the sixth rank will always win, despite the drawing power of the Bishops on opposite colors. (The only exception is in certain cases where a Rook Pawn is involved.)

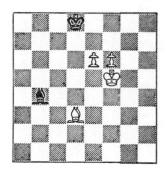

	WHITE	BLACK
1	......	K—K1

Else White plays B—N5 cutting off any contact of Black's King with the threatened area (see next note).

	WHITE	BLACK
2	B—N5ch	K—B1

If 2 ...... K—Q1; 3 K—N6, B—R6; 4 K—B7 and 5 P—K7ch winning.

	WHITE	BLACK
3	K—K4!	B—R6

The Bishop must stay on its present diagonal to guard against P—K7ch. White's King can therefore head for Queen 7.

	WHITE	BLACK
4	K—Q5	B—N5
5	K—B6	B—R6
6	K—Q7	B—N5
7	P—K7ch	Resigns

White must queen.

Diagram 243

White to move.

In endings with Bishops on opposite colors, where a player has two connected passed Pawns on the fifth rank, the possibility of winning pivots on the question of whether one of the Pawns can advance successfully to the sixth rank.

In this case the ending is a draw because (1) P—Q6ch is always answered by ...... B×P and (2) White's King cannot maneuver to Queen Bishop 5. And of course after P—K6 White can make no headway.

	WHITE	BLACK
1	B—R3	B—B2
2	K—K4	B—N1
3	K—B5	B—B2

However, if the Black Bishop is placed at Queen Rook 6 to begin with, White wins: 1 K—B4!, K—K1 (if 1 ...... B—N7; 2 P—Q6ch and 3 K—Q5 wins); 2 P—Q6, K—Q1; 3 K—Q5, K—K1; 4 P—K6 etc.

Diagram 244

Black to move.

If the White Pawns were on white squares, Black would have complete sway over the black squares and could draw easily with ...... B—Q3 or K—B3.

But, as matters stand, White has a win because his Pawns are on black squares; and because his pieces are in complete control of the white squares, making possible a decisive invasion by his King.

	WHITE	BLACK
1	......	B—B1
2	B—B4ch!	K—K2

Black has hopes of 3 P—B5?, B—N2! drawing as in the previous example.

	WHITE	BLACK
3	K—K4!	B—N2
4	K—B5	B—R3
5	K—N4!	B—N2

Or 5 ...... K—K1; 6 P—B5, K—K2; 7 P—B6ch, K—Q1; 8 K—B5 followed by K—N6—B7 and wins.

	WHITE	BLACK
6	K—N5!	K—B1
7	K—N6	B—R1
8	K—R7	B—N2
9	B—N3! and wins	

White wins the Bishop. It is curious that the Pawns never moved.

Bishop and Pawn Endings ■ 209

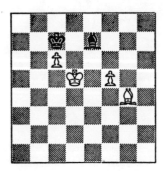

Diagram 245

White to move.
Given Bishops on opposite colors, a player with two passed Pawns that are two or more files apart will win. The weaker side's King has too much ground to cover.

	WHITE	BLACK
1	B—B3!	B—R5
2	K—K6	K—Q1
3	P—B6	B—N4

Black's King must stay close to the Queen Bishop Pawn.

	WHITE	BLACK
4	P—KB7	B—R3
5	K—B6	B—B1
6	K—N6	K—K2
7	K—R7	K—Q1

If 7 ...... K×P; 8 P—B7 wins.

	WHITE	BLACK
8	K—N8	K—K2
9	P—B7 and wins	

Diagram 246

White to move.
The only difference between this and the previous position is that White's King Bishop Pawn has been replaced by a King Pawn. But this narrows the Black King's defensive front to manageable limits.

	WHITE	BLACK
1	B—B3	B—R5
2	K—K6	B—N4
3	K—B7	B—R5

            4   P—K6   K—Q1
                Drawn

Because Black's King commands the critical squares King 2
and Queen Bishop 2, Black can draw, for example 5 P—K7ch,
B×P; 6 P—B7ch, K×P etc.

Knight and Pawn Endings

Here too the basic problem is the queening of a Pawn. The
forces often work at close quarters because of the Knight's
short hop. There is much finesse here which shows the powers
of the Knight in their best, as well as their worst, light.

Diagram 247

White to move.
*Here the win is possible because
the immediate advance of the
Pawn ties down Black's pieces.*

            WHITE   BLACK
        1   P—N6   N—N2
        2   N—Q6   N—R4

On 2 . . . . . . N—B4 White has the same winning reply.

        3   K—B8!   N—N2
        4   N—B7 mate

On the other hand, if Black moves first in the diagram position he can prevent the advance of the Pawn and eventually
force a draw by invoking a stalemate possibility: 1 . . . . . .
N—B5!; 2 N—K3, K—R2; 3 N—N4, K—R1; 4 N—K5,
K—R2; 5 N—Q7, K—R1; 6 N—B6 (it now seems as if White
can win, for example 6 . . . . . . N—R4?; 7 P—N6 etc.), N—N3!
and White can make no headway, as 7 K×N stalemates Black.

Knight and Pawn Endings   ■   211

Diagram 248

Black to move.
White, who is a Pawn up, must maneuver patiently to win both remaining Black Pawns in return for his Queen Pawn. Then the win will be a matter of time.

	WHITE	BLACK
1	......	K—K1
2	N—Q5!	K—Q2
3	N×Pch	K×P
4	P—K5ch!	K—K2
5	N—Q5ch	K—Q2

If now 6 K×P?, K—K3 wins a Pawn.

6	P—K6ch	K—Q3
7	P—K7	K—Q2
8	K×P	N—K5ch
9	K—B5	N—Q3ch
10	K—K5	N—B2ch
11	K—B6	N—Q3
12	P—N5	Resigns

The finish might be 12 ...... N—K5ch; 13 K—B5, N—Q3ch; 14 K—K5, N—B2ch; 15 K—B6, N—Q3; 16 P—N6 and wins.

Bishop against Knight Endings

Bishop and Knight, as we know from the table of relative values, are of equal value. Nevertheless there are many positions in which the Bishop is superior. This is especially true when there are Pawns on both wings.

This follows because the Bishop, being a long-range piece, moves easily from one zone to another. The Knight on the other hand moves in comparatively short hops and takes several moves to get from one side of the board to another. This contrast in mobility may often make all the difference.

Nevertheless there are also situations in which the Knight shows to immense advantage. This happens for the most part when the Bishop travels on the same color as that on which all or most of his Pawns are placed. Such a Pawn position is highly disadvantageous because the mobility of the Bishop is seriously hampered, while the Bishop's disabilities are further underlined by the necessity for his guarding the Pawns. The Knight will almost invariably win these endings.

Diagram 249

White to move.
A radical example of a vastly superior Bishop.

WHITE	BLACK
1 B—K5!	K—K1

Black is helpless. If 1 ...... N—B3; 2 B×N, K×B; 3 K×P with an easy win for White. Thus the Knight remains useless.

2 K×P	K—K2

3	K—N7	K—K3
4	P—B6!	K×B
5	P—B7	Resigns

Diagram 250

White to move.
White's first move, stalemating the Knight, leads to an easy win against Black's helpless forces.

	WHITE	BLACK
1	B—Q5!	K—K2
2	K—B5	K—K1

If 2 ...... K—Q2; 3 K—B6, K—K1; 4 P—K6, K—B1; 5 P—K7ch, K—K1; 6 K—K6 and White mates next move.

3	K—K6	K—B1
4	K—Q7 and wins	

The Pawn must queen.

Diagram 251

White to move.
The Knight is handicapped in stopping a passed Rook Pawn because its mobility decreases sharply at the edge of the board. In this example the Black King, being well behind the Pawn, is equally useless.

	WHITE	BLACK
1	K—N5!	N—B7
2	P—R4!	N—K5ch

214 ■ Lesson 12—Endgames

Or 2 ...... N—N5; 3 P—R5 and Black loses because he must move his Knight.

3	K—N6	N×B
4	P—R5	N—B5
5	P—R6	N—K4ch
6	K—N7	K—B5

Black is one tempo short of being able to play ...... N—N3.

7	P—R7	Resigns

Black is helpless.

Diagram 252

White to move.
Black's Knight is badly placed for stopping the White Pawn and cannot be successfully supported by Black's King. The Bishop, on the other hand, plays an effective role.

	WHITE	BLACK
1	B—B3!	......

Of course not 1 K×N??, K×P and Black draws. Nor would 1 B—K5? do because of 1 ...... K—N3; 2 B—Q4ch, K—N4 and Black can hold his own.

1	......	K—N3
2	B—R5ch!	K—N4

If 2 ...... K×B; 3 K×N wins.

3	B—Q8	K—B4
4	B—R4	K—N4
5	B—N5	K—B4
6	B—K3ch	K—Q4
7	B—Q4!	N—Q3

Forced, as any King move allows the winning reply 8 K×N.

8	P—B7! and wins	

Black must submit to the loss of his Knight, whereupon the Pawn queens.

Diagram 253

White to move.
Black has a far advanced passed Pawn and his Bishop has considerable mobility. It takes delicate maneuvering with the Black King and Bishop to achieve a win.

	WHITE	BLACK
1	N—K2	B—K6!

Black needs to get his Bishop to King 8 to win. At this point White dares not play 2 K×B because 2 ...... K—N7 ensures the winning advance of the Rook Pawn.

	WHITE	BLACK
2	N—N3	B—Q7!

And now if 3 N—B1ch, K—N8; 4 N×B, P—R7 wins; or 3 K—B2, B—K8ch! winning.

	WHITE	BLACK
3	N—K2	B—K8!
4	N—Q4	K—R8!
5	N—K2	P—R7
6	N—Q4	K—N8
7	N—K2ch	K—B8
8	N—N3ch	B×N
9	K×B	P—R8/R! and wins

White is stalemated after 9 ...... P—R8/Q?

Diagram 254

Diagram 254

Black to move.
*Black is not only a Pawn
ahead; his vastly superior
Bishop can stalemate the
Knight.*

	WHITE	BLACK
1	......	B—B5!

Taking away all the Knight's moves.

	WHITE	BLACK
2	K—N4	K—Q4
3	K—B3	K—B4 and wins

Another way was 3 ...... P—K5 with an easy win.

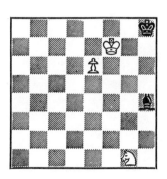

Diagram 255

White to move.
*The Bishop is on the short
diagonal and Black's King is
very unfavorably placed. A win
for White is indicated, though
the method is subtle.*

	WHITE	BLACK
1	N—B3	B—Q1
2	N—K5	K—R2
3	N—N4	K—R1
4	N—B6 and wins	

If 4 ...... B—B2 (or the like); 5 P—K7 and the Pawn
queens. Or 4 ...... B×N; 5 K×B and the Pawn will queen.

Bishop against Knight Endings ■ 217

Diagram 256

White to move.

When the passed Pawn is already at the seventh rank, the unassisted Bishop is helpless. This is because the Knight can simultaneously command the queening square (Queen 8) and also the blockading square (King 7).

	WHITE	BLACK
1	N—B6	K—K7
2	K—Q6	K—K6
3	N—K7	B—N6ch
4	K—B6 and wins	

The Bishop is blocked off.

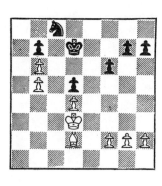

Diagram 257

Black to move.

White's Bishop has no targets for attack. Furthermore, it is hemmed in by White Pawns on black squares; an additional drawback of White's game is that he is helpless on the white squares.

	WHITE	BLACK
1	......	N—Q3!

Stronger than the obvious 1 ...... N×P, as Black will now win both doubled Pawns.

	WHITE	BLACK
2	B—N4	N×P
3	B—B8	P—N3
4	P—N4	N—Q3!

218 ■ Lesson 12—Endgames

If now 5 B×N, K×B followed by ...... K—B3 with an easy win for Black.

5	P—R4	N—B1
6	B—B5	K—B3
7	K—K3	N×P
8	B—K7	N—Q2

Black will soon be ready to advance his new passed Pawn.

9	P—R5	K—N4!
10	K—Q3	K—R5
11	K—B3	P—QN4!
12	P—B3	P—B4!

Black frees his Knight.

13	NP×P	P×BP
14	P—R6	N—N1
15	K—Q3	N—B3
16	B—N5	P—N5
17	B—Q2	N—Q1
	Resigns	

After 18 K—B2, N—K3; 19 B—K3, K—R6 White can stop the passed Pawn only at the cost of losing his Queen Pawn.

The Two Bishops

This section deals with endings in which one player has two Bishops while the other has a Bishop and Knight, or two Knights.

According to the table of relative values, the Bishop and Knight are of equal value. But the co-operation of a Bishop-pair is something that cannot be weighed in the scales. These co-operating Bishops, with their potential control over every square on the board, confer a number of advantages on their possessor. These include:

1. The Bishops can cut down the Knight's mobility enormously.

2. They can support the aggressive advance of their own King and reduce the mobility of the opposing King.

3. In addition the possessor of the Bishops can further immobilize the Knight by appropriate Pawn moves.

4. One of the great reserve powers of the Bishops is the possibility of simplifying via exchanges into a more easily won ending.

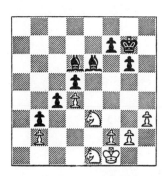

Diagram 258

Black to move.
A powerful demonstration of the superior striking power of the Bishops, this time by liquidation.

	WHITE	BLACK
1	......	B—R6!

If now 2 P×B, P—N7 and White cannot stop the Queen Knight Pawn from queening.

	WHITE	BLACK
2	N—Q1	B×NP!
3	N×B	P—B6

Now 4 N/N2—Q3 will not do because of 4 ...... P—N7, and Black's Pawn queens.

	WHITE	BLACK
4	N/K1—Q3	B—B4!

Threatens 5 ...... B×Nch; 6 N×B, P—N7 and wins.

	WHITE	BLACK
5	K—K2	B×Nch!
6	K×B	P×N
	Resigns	

White's King is helpless.

Diagram 259

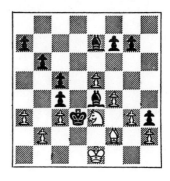

White to move.

White is helpless against the far-ranging Bishops, and can only mark time as Black advances his Queen-side Pawns in order to create a passed Pawn. Black's aggressively placed King plays a useful role.

	WHITE	BLACK
1	P—KN4	P—QN4
2	P—N5	P—R4
3	K—Q1	P—N5
4	BP×P	BP×P
5	P×P	P×P
6	N—B2	P—B6

Black avoids 6 . . . . . . P—N6??, 7 N—K1 mate.

	WHITE	BLACK
7	P×P	. . . . . .

Or 7 K—B1, P—N6; 8 N—Q4, B—R6!; 9 P×B, P—N7ch and the Pawn queens.

	WHITE	BLACK
7	. . . . . .	P—N6
	Resigns	

After 8 N—Q4 or N—K3 Black plays 8 . . . . . . P—N7 and the Pawn cannot be stopped. A fine example of the power of the united Bishops.

LESSON 13:
ENDGAMES WITH ROOKS

Rook and Pawn Endings

Rooks are par excellence the pieces that thrive on open lines. Place them on an open file or on the seventh rank and they are devastating. Correspondingly, place them on a line where they have little scope, and they are at a serious disadvantage.

Rook and Pawn endings are the most common type of ending and it is therefore well worth while to have a good understanding of them. These endings revolve to a considerable degree around the struggle to queen a passed Pawn.

If you are the player who has the passed Pawn, your correct procedure is to place your Rook behind the Pawn. This gives added impetus to the Pawn's threat to advance to the queening square.

If your opponent is the one who has the passed Pawn, it is still correct strategy to place your Rook behind the Pawn. If you place your Rook in front of the Pawn, the Rook's freedom of action can be reduced to the vanishing point.

Even more so than in most endings the King plays a very important role here. The cooperation of King, Rook and Pawn is often the key to victory.

Diagram 260

White to move.

This is the basic winning position in the ending of Rook and Pawn vs. Rook. White's first move drives Black's King away in order to give the White King elbow room.

WHITE	BLACK
1 R—QB1ch	K—N2

And now playing out the White King directly is not enough to win: 2 K—Q7, R—Q7ch; 3 K—K6, R—K7ch; 4 K—Q6, R—Q7ch; 5 K—K5, R—K7ch etc. Hence White's next move, which will enable him to shield his King from checks.

	WHITE	BLACK
2	R—B4!	R—B8
3	K—Q7	R—Q8ch
4	K—K6	R—K8ch
5	K—B6	R—KB8ch
6	K—K5	R—K8ch
7	R—K4! and wins	

Black has no more checks.

Diagram 261

White to move.

Black is safe so long as the two Kings face each other and Black's King cannot be checked.

WHITE	BLACK
1 K—B4	. . . . . .

Threatening to win with 2 R—QN8ch and 3 P—R8/Q.

1	K—B7

If 1 ...... R—QB8ch; 2 K—Q3, R—Q8ch; 3 K—K2 and wins.

2	K—Q4	K—Q7
3	K—K4	K—K7
4	K—B5!	K—B6

Or 4 ...... R—KB8ch; 5 K—N4, R—KN8ch; 6 K—R3, R—KR8ch; 7 K—N2 and wins.

5	R—KB8!	R×P
6	K—N6 dis ch and wins	

Black's Rook is lost.

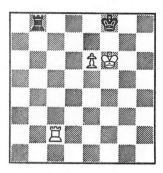

Diagram 262

Black to move.
If Black's Rook were at Queen Knight 8 he could now draw with 1 ...... R—KB8ch etc. But with his Rook badly placed, he is lost.

	WHITE	BLACK
1	......	R—R1

If 1 ...... K—N1; 2 R—KN2ch, K—B1; 3 P—K7ch, K—K1; 4 R—N8ch wins for White.

2	R—KR2	K—N1
3	R—KN2ch	K—R1

If 3 ...... K—B1; 4 P—K7ch wins.

4	K—B7	R—R2ch
5	P—K7 and wins	

Analogous situations with a Knight Pawn or Rook Pawn are drawn. See Diagram 263.

Diagram 263

Black to move.

Despite the similarity between this position and Diagram 262, White has a draw here.

	WHITE	BLACK
1	......	R—R7
2	R—Q1	R—KN7ch

If now 3 K—B1?, K—R7; 4 R—Q8, R—KB7ch; 5 K—K1, K—N8 and Black wins.

	WHITE	BLACK
3	K—R1	R—KR7ch
4	K—N1	Drawn

The theoretically indicated 4 ...... P—N7? loses because of 5 R—B3ch.

Diagram 264

White to move.

A valuable practical position for drawing against the extra Pawn when the defender's King and Rook are placed to advantage.

Black keeps his Rook on the third rank until the Pawn reaches that row. Then the Black Rook goes to the eighth rank to check the White King, which can no longer be shielded by its own Pawn. This makes it impossible for White to win.

	WHITE	BLACK
1	R—Q2	K—N2
2	K—N5	R—QB3
3	P—B5	R—QN3
4	R—QR2	R—Q3
5	R—R7ch	K—N1
6	P—B6	R—Q8!

The correct procedure. If instead 6 ...... R—Q1?; 7 K—N6! and Black has no defense to the threat of 8 R—KN7ch, K—B1 (or 8 ...... K—R1; 9 R—KR7ch, K—N1; 10 P—B7ch, K—B1; 11 R—R8ch and wins); 9 R—KR7!, K—N1; 10 P—B7ch, K—B1; 11 R—R8ch, K—K2; 12 R×R, K×R; 13 P—B8/Qch and wins.

7	K—N6	R—KN8ch
8	K—B5	K—B1
9	K—K6	R—K8ch
10	K—B5	K—N1
	Drawn	

Whenever White's King goes to the sixth rank, Black checks. This prevents White from making any headway.

Diagram 265

White to move.
White can win if he can escape the checks (if   K—B8, R—R1ch etc.).

	WHITE	BLACK
1	K—B6	R—R3ch

If now 2 K—K5?, R—KN3 followed by ...... K—R3 and Black draws.

	WHITE	BLACK
2	K—B5!	R—R4ch

But not 2 ...... R—KN3??; 3 P—N8/Q!, R×Q; 4 R—KR7 mate.

	WHITE	BLACK
3	K—B4	R—R5ch

If 3 ...... R—KN4; 4 R—B5 wins.

	WHITE	BLACK
4	K—B3!	R—R6ch

If 4 ...... R—KN5; 5 R—B5ch!, K—R5; 6 R—B4 wins.

	WHITE	BLACK
5	K—N2	R—R7ch
6	R—B2!	R—R1

But now White's Rook gets to King Bishop 8.

	WHITE	BLACK
7	R—B8	R—R7ch
8	K—B3!	R—R6ch
9	K—K4	R—R5ch
10	K—Q5	R—R4ch
11	K—B6	R—R3ch
12	K—N7	Resigns

Black has no further resources.

Diagram 266

White to move.
*Despite the reduced nature of
the material White can win—
though only by a series of
remarkable finesses.*

	WHITE	BLACK
1	R—QR7ch	K—N5
2	P—N7	R—QN3

Now 3 K—Q5 is useless because of 3 ...... K—N4; while
3 R—R1 is answered by 3 ...... K—B4.

3	K—Q4!	R—Q3ch

Whereas now if 3 ...... K—N4; 4 K—Q5, K—N5; 5 R—R1!
and Black is helpless against the coming R—QN1ch.

4	K—K5	R—QN3
5	R—R1!	K—B6

If 5 ...... K—B4; 6 R—QB1ch, K—N5; 7 R—QN1ch and
wins.

6	R—QB1ch	K—N7
7	R—B7	K—N6
8	K—Q5	K—N5

If 8 ...... R—N4ch; 9 K—B6 wins.

9	R—B1	K—R6

If 8 ...... K—R4 or ...... K—R5; 9 R—QR1ch wins.

10	R—QR1ch	K—N7

Forced.

11	R—R7! and wins	

If 11 ...... K—N6; 12 K—B5, R—N5; 13 R—R1 and
Black is helpless against the coming R—QN1ch.

Diagram 267

Black to move.
*To make his advantage tell,
Black must resort to a whole
series of finesses.*

	WHITE	BLACK
1	......	K—K4!

Threatening to win by means of ...... K—K5—Q6 and thus forcing White's King to the third rank.

2	K—B3	K—Q3!
3	R—B8	K—Q2!
4	R—B4	P—N4!

Black has gained valuable time, and 5 R—Q4ch, K—B3; 6 R—Q3 is now ruled out because of 6 ...... P—N5 and wins.

5	R—B5	P—N5
6	K—K4	P—N6!

Not 6 ...... R×P; 7 R×R, P×R; 8 K—Q3 followed by 9 K×P and White draws against the Rook Pawn. Likewise if 6 ...... P×P; 7 K—Q3 and the position is a book draw.

7	K—Q3	P—R4

If now 8 K—B4, P—N7; 9 R—QN5, R—R5ch; 10 K—Q3, R—QN5!; 11 R×R, P×R; 12 K—B2, P×P and wins.

8	P—B4	P—N7 dis ch
9	K—B2	R—QN6!
10	K—N1	P—R5
11	R—QR5	P—R6
12	R—R6	R—R6
	Resigns	

If 13 R—QN6, R—R8ch; 14 K—B2, R—QB8ch (or 14 ...... P—R7) wins for Black.

Rook and Pawn Endings ▪ 229

Diagram 268

White to move.

White wins with ease, as he can bring his King over to support the advance of his passed Pawn, whereas Black's King is cut off by the White Rook.

	WHITE	BLACK
1	K—B2	P—R4

If now 2 K—K3?, K—K4! and Black's King gets to the scene of action.

2	K—K1!	P—N4
3	K—Q2	K—B4
4	K—Q3	R—R1
5	P—B4	R—Q1ch
6	K—B3	R—QB1

This stops P—B5, so White advances his King.

7	K—N4	R—QN1ch
8	K—R5	R—QB1
9	K—N5	R—QN1ch
10	K—R6	R—QB1

Now White gives up his blockade of Black's King in order to support the advance of the passed Pawn.

11	R—QB2!	K—K4
12	K—N7!	R—B4
13	K—N6 !	Resigns

For if 13 ...... R—B1; 14 P—B5 followed by P—B6 and P—B7 and K—N7 wins for White.

Diagram 269

Black to move.
White threatens to obtain an easily won King and Pawn ending with R—Q7ch! followed by P—K6ch.

	WHITE	BLACK
1	......	K—K2
2	P—K6	R—R5

White again threatened by R—Q7ch etc.

| 3 | P—N5! | ...... |

In order to play K—N6 later without allowing ...... R×Pch in reply.

3	......	P×P
4	R—Q7ch	K—B1
5	R—KB7ch!	K—N1

If 5 ...... K—K1; 6 R×P gives White an easy win.

6	K—N6	P—N5
7	P—R6!!	P×P
8	P—K7	R—R1

If 8 ...... R—R3ch; 9 R—B6 wins for White.

| 9 | R—B6 | Resigns |

Black has no defense to the coming 10 R—Q6 and 11 R—Q8ch. (If 9 ...... R—K1; 10 R—Q6! still wins.)

Diagram 270

White to move.
White uses a mate threat to force an easily won King and Pawn ending.

	WHITE	BLACK
1	K—B6!	R—KB8ch

White threatened R—KR8 mate.

2	K—N7!	R—B7
3	R—KR8ch	K—N4
4	R—KB8!	Resigns

Black must exchange Rooks (if 4 ...... R×P??; 5 R—B5 mate); but after 4 ...... R×R; 5 K×R, K—B3; 6 K—K8 White has an easy win: 6 ...... K—N3; 7 K—Q7, K—B2; 8 K×P, K—K2; 9 K—B6 winning the Queen Pawn.

Diagram 271

Black to move.

Each player has a wing majority of Pawns. But while White's is immobilized, Black's King-side majority can be set in motion, yielding an eventual passed Pawn and an open file for his Rook.

	WHITE	BLACK
1	......	P—R3!
2	R—K3	P—N4
3	P×P	P×P
4	R—N3	R—B1!
5	R—K3	R—KR1

The Rook is very formidable on this file.

6	R—K2	P—B5
7	P×P	P×P
8	K—B2	R—R7!

If now 9 K—Q2, P—K6ch!; 10 P×Pch, P×Pch; 11 K—Q1, R×R; 12 K×R, K—K5 and White is helpless against the passed Pawn: 13 K—K1, K—Q6; 14 K—Q1, P—K7ch; 15 K—K1, K—K6; 16 P—R4, P×P and Black queens first with checkmate.

9	K—N3	R—R6ch!
10	K—N2	R—Q6
11	R—B2	P—B6
12	K—B1	P—K6!

Obtaining a passed Pawn which is immediately decisive.

13	P×Pch	K×P
	Resigns	

There is no defense to the coming ...... P—B7 etc.

Rook and Pawn Endings ■ 233

Rooks and Minor Pieces

In endings in which each player has a Rook and minor piece, the result is usually determined by the minor pieces. For example: in an ending of Rook and Bishop against Rook and Knight, the outcome is likely to be the same as it would be without the Rooks. If the Knight is superior, then the Rook and Knight will triumph over the Rook and Bishop. If the Bishop is superior, then the Rook and Bishop will doubtless triumph over the Rook and Knight.

In a sense, adding the efforts of a minor piece to those of a Rook is like adding apples and oranges—or at least this is likely to be the view of the inexperienced player. In actual practice it works out differently, for the co-operation of Rooks and minor pieces creates many beautiful and powerful effects. In any event, the goal is still the same: the supported advance of a Pawn to the queening square.

The endings in which a player has the advantage of the Exchange are particularly instructive; for they demonstrate in the clearest possible way the superiority of a Rook over a minor piece.

On the other hand, if the minor piece is supported by two strongly placed Pawns, the relationship is reversed. In that event, the Rook will be helpless against the powerful Pawns.

Diagram 272

White to move.

White wins even though he must lose back his extra Pawn.

	WHITE	BLACK
1	P—R4!!	R×P

Or 1 ...... P—R3; 2 P—R5, R×P; 3 R—B6 and White wins.

	WHITE	BLACK
2	R—N5!	R×R
3	BP×R	B—Q6
4	B—B6	K—N1
5	P—R5	K—B1
6	P—R6	Resigns

Black must give up his Bishop to stop White from queening a Pawn by 7 P—N6 etc.

Diagram 273

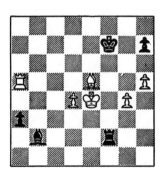

Black to move.

At first sight it seems that Black can hold the game because White's Rook has to stand guard over Black's far-advanced Queen Rook Pawn. But White overcomes the difficulty with a mating attack.

	WHITE	BLACK
1	......	P—R3
2	K—Q5!	B—B8

Rook and Minor Piece Endings ■ 235

3	R—R7ch	K—N1

If 3 ...... K—K1; 4 K—K6! wins at once.

4	K—K6!	B—N7
5	R—KN7ch!	K—B1
6	R—KR7!	K—K1

Else 7 R—R8 mate.

7	R—R7!	Resigns

Black has no resource against the threat of R—R8 mate.

Diagram 274

Black to move.

To win an ending with Bishops on opposite colors, some ingenious finesse is usually required. So here: instead of winning two Pawns, Black wisely contents himself with one.

WHITE	BLACK
1	R × RP!!

Black avoids 1 ...... R × BPch followed by ...... R × RP, for in that case White's Bishop can take a hand in the fight that will center around the advance of Black's Rook Pawn.

2	B—Q6	R—R8ch
3	K—B2	P—R5
4	R—R7	R—R7ch!

Good timing. After 5 K—K3 White's King would be too far from the passed Pawn. So the King must go to the first rank, where it will be exposed to Black's threats.

5	K—B1	P—R6

Black's judgment will be vindicated. His Bishop plays an important role in supporting the advance of the passed Pawn, whereas White's Bishop does not participate at all.

6	R—K7ch	K—Q1

         7 R—KR7   R—R7!
              Resigns

If 8 R×P, B—N7ch wins the Rook. Or 8 K—N1, R—
KN7ch; 9 K—B1 (not 9 K—R1, R—N2 dis ch etc.), P—R7
and White has no defense to the coming ...... R—N8ch.

Diagram 275

White to move.
White's powerful passed Pawn
wins very quickly.

              WHITE   BLACK
         1 P—Q7!   ......
Threatening 2 R—K8ch or 2 N×P.
         1 ......   N—Q1
If 1 ...... R—Q1; 2 R—K8ch, K—R2 (or 2 ...... K—
N2; 3 N—K6ch); 3 N—K6, R×P; 4 N—B8ch wins.
         2 R—K8ch   K—B2
         3 N×P!   N×N
         4 R×R   Resigns

As 4 ...... N×R would allow the Pawn to queen, White
has an easy win.

Diagram 276

Black to move.
*Black's extra Pawn wins very
quickly for him, as his passed
Pawn is a formidable weapon
and his Knight has interesting
forking possibilities.*

WHITE	BLACK
1	P—B6!

Threatens 2 ...... P—B7!; 3 R×P, R×N!; 4 K×R,
N—K5ch followed by 5 ...... N×R with a piece ahead.

| 2 R—R1 | P—B7! |

And if now 3 K—Q3, R—KR4; 4 R—R1, R×P! wins a
Pawn.

3 R—KB1	N—B4ch!
4 K—Q3	R×Nch!
5 ` K×R	N—K6
6 R×P	N—Q8ch
7 K—Q4	N×R

Now White still has some drawing hopes before Black's
King can get to the other side.

8 P—R4	N—N5
9 K—K4	P—R3
10 K—B4	N—B3!
11 K—K5	P—N4!
12 P×P	P×P

If now 13 K×N, P—N5 and the Pawn queens.

| 13 K—B5 | P—N5 |

And Black wins by bringing his King over to support the
advance of his Pawn, after winning White's Pawn.

Diagram 277

Black to move.
*White's passed Pawn wins the
ending for him.*

WHITE	BLACK
1	K—Q2

Or 1 ...... N—B5; 2 P—R7, R—R1; 3 R×Nch, P×R;
4 B—N2 and wins.

| 2 P—R7 | R—R1 |
| 3 B—N2!! | P—B3 |

Other Pawn moves also lose to 4 R—KR3. If 3 ...... R—
R1; 4 R—B7ch!, K×R; 5 B×R and Black cannot stop the
Pawn from queening.

| 4 R—KR3 | R—R1 |
| 5 B×P | Resigns |

Black loses his Rook.

Diagram 278

White to move.
*White, who is already a Pawn
ahead, forces the win of a
second Pawn.*

WHITE	BLACK
1 B—B7!	......

Threatening 2 R×N and also 2 B×P. Black dare not play
1 ...... R×B?? because of 2 R—K8 mate.

Rook and Minor Piece Endings ■ 239

| 1 ...... | N—Q5 |
| 2 R×P | Resigns |

Black still cannot play ...... R×B, and he will soon lose a third Pawn.

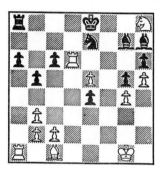

Diagram 279

Black to move.
White is momentarily the Exchange ahead, as 1 ......
B×N? is answered by
2 R×KRP when White wins
a piece.

Black can arrange to win the piece but White maintains a decisive advantage.

WHITE	BLACK
1	N—B1
2 R×BP	B×N
3 R×KRP	R—R2

Thus Black can retain the piece, but he is helpless against White's magnificently active forces.

| 4 B—K3! | R—Q2 |
| 5 QR×P! | K—B1 |

If 5 ...... B×P; 6 QR—K6ch wins a piece. Or 5 ...... K—Q1; 6 B×Pch, K—K1; 7 P—K6 and wins.

6 R—R8!	R—QB2
7 R×B!	R×R
8 R×Nch	Resigns

White's material advantage wins easily for him.

Diagram 280

White to move.

Black's Bishop has the job of protecting two weak Pawns. White now forces Black to give up the protection of one of the Pawns.

	WHITE	BLACK
1	R—QB6ch!!	K—Q2

Or 1 ...... K—N2; 2 R—B4, B—N7; 3 R—K4, B—B3; 4 R—K6, B—Q5; 5 R—Q6! and White wins a Pawn.

	WHITE	BLACK
2	R—B4!	B—B4
3	R—KN4!	K—K2
4	R×Pch	K—B3
5	R—N6ch	K×P
6	R×RP	Resigns

For 7 R×P wins easily for White.

Diagram 281

White to move.

White can win by simplifying into a won King and Pawn ending. However, he must not do this by 1 K—K5 dis ch, K—K2; 2 R×P, B×Rch; 3 K×B, K—B3 as Black has the Opposition and can therefore draw.

	WHITE	BLACK
1	R—B5!	......

White threatens mate. If 1 ...... K—K1; 2 K—N7! followed by 3 R—K5ch (driving Black's King to the Queen file) followed by 4 R—K4 and then K—N6—B5. White can then play R×P, simplifying into a won King and Pawn ending, as Black cannot get the Opposition.

1	. . . . . .	K—N1
2	R—B8ch!	K—R2
3	K—B7!	Resigns

After 3 . . . . . . K—R3; 4 R—KN8! Black's King is limited to the King Rook file. White plays 5 R—N4 followed by K—B6—B5 and then R×P, winning as previously shown.

Diagram 282

White to move.
White has only one Pawn for the Exchange, but his pieces are well placed and his two connected passed Pawns are formidable.

	WHITE	BLACK
1	B—B5!	R—Q1
2	R—Q1	N—B2
3	R×Rch	N×R
4	B—Q6	. . . . . .

White has simplified to the point where he is now ready to force the winning advance of his Queen Bishop Pawn.

| 4 | . . . . . . | R—B2 |
| 5 | P—B7 | R×QBP |

Black has no choice.

6 B×R and wins

White is a piece to the good.

Diagram 283

White to move.

In the long run White is helpless against the Black Pawns.

	WHITE	BLACK
1	R—N8ch	K—B7
2	K—B2	K—K7
3	R—K8ch	K—B8!
4	R—KB8	P—B7
5	R—B7	. . . . . .

White can only mark time.

5	. . . . . .	K—K7
6.	R—K7ch	K—B6
7	R—KB7ch	B—B5
	Resigns	

The Bishop Pawn must queen.

LESSON 14:

ENDGAMES WITH QUEENS, SURVEY OF THE OPENINGS, AND A QUIZ-REVIEW

Endings in which the Queens are still present are seen rather infrequently. They are difficult to handle, primarily because of the Queen's considerable powers. In an ending of Queen and Pawn against Queen, for example, the weaker side generally has recourse to innumerable checks. These not only strain the other player's patience—they also make his victory doubtful.

The proper stratagem against these almost endless checking possibilities is a paradoxical one. Instead of placing one's King as far away as possible from the hostile Queen, it is preferable to bring the King rather close in, as this cuts down the checking possibilities. But the best remedy of all is to use the checking power of one's own Queen to force, or threaten to force, an exchange of Queens.

Against weaker units the Queen displays the proverbial powers of divergent checks that must prove irresistible. The endings of Queen against a far-advanced Pawn offer a special field of study that calls for foresight and finesses.

Diagram 284

Black to move.

With the Queens still on the board, it is doubtful whether White can win. But White plays to force the exchange of Queens, after which he wins by capturing Black's remaining Pawn and promoting one of his own Pawns.

	WHITE	BLACK
1	......	K—B2
2	Q—Q7ch!	K—N1

If 2 ...... K—B1 (or to the third rank); 3 Q—Q6ch! wins.
If 2 ...... K—R1 White wins with 3 Q—B8ch! and 4 Q—N7ch!

	WHITE	BLACK
3	Q—B8ch!	K—B2
4	Q—N7ch!	Resigns

The King and Pawn ending is an easy win for White.

Diagram 285

White to move.

White wins by a series of Queen checks which bring this powerful piece to King Knight 8.

	WHITE	BLACK
1	Q—R4ch	K—N1
2	Q—KB4ch	K—R1
3	Q—B8	K—N1
4	Q—Q6ch!	K—R1

Queen Endings ■ 245

5 Q—R3ch!   . . . . . .

This gets the Queen to King Knight 8.

     5 . . . . . .   K—N1

     6 Q—KN3ch   K—R1

     7 Q—N8 and wins

Black cannot guard against the threat of Q×B mate and save his Rook at the same time.

Diagram 286

White to move.

To win, White must give up his Queen for the Rook and Knight, remaining with a won King and Pawn ending.

WHITE	BLACK
1 Q—R4!	R—B2
2 Q—KN4ch!	K—Q1

If 2 . . . . . . K—K2; 3 Q—K6ch wins more rapidly. If 2 . . . . . . K—K1; 3 K—Q6! is decisive.

3 Q—N8ch	K—Q2
4 Q—K6ch	K—Q1
5 Q×N!	R×Q
6 K×R and wins	

Diagram 287

Black to move.

*While material is
approximately even, White is
lost because Black's pieces are
well posted to exploit the
unfortunate position of the
White King.*

	WHITE	BLACK
1	. . . . . .	Q—B6ch
2	B—N3	P—N4!

If now 3 R—Q6ch, K—B2; 4 R—Q7ch, K—K1; 5 R—Q2,
Q—B8ch; 6 R—KN2, P—R4!; 7 P×P, Q×P mate. This
clever mating motif turns up in the actual play as well.

3	P×P e.p.	K—N4
4	R—Q2	P—R4!
5	P×P	Q—B8ch
6	R—KN2	Q—B4 mate

Diagram 288

White to move.

Black threatens to draw by queening his Pawn. But the Queen can always win against a Knight Pawn (or a King Pawn or a Queen Pawn) by forcing the hostile King in front of the Pawn.

	WHITE	BLACK
1	Q—N8	K—R7
2	Q—R7ch	K—N6
3	Q—N6ch	K—B7
4	Q—B5ch	K—Q7
5	Q—N4ch	K—B7
6	Q—B4ch	K—Q7
7	Q—N3	K—B8
8	Q—QB3ch	K—N8

Now White's King has time to approach, so that a mating position can be built up.

9	K—K3!	K—R7
10	Q—B2	K—R8
11	Q—R4ch	K—N8

Now 12 K—Q2?? stalemates Black. But 12 K—Q3!, K—B8; 13 Q—B2 mate is an alternative winning method.

12	K—K2!	K—B8
13	Q—Q1 mate	

Diagram 289

White to move.
In positions of this kind, the Rook Pawn draws against the Queen.

WHITE	BLACK
1 Q—KN3ch	K—R1
Drawn	

If White moves his Queen to lift the stalemate, the Black King comes out of the corner, again threatening to queen. The stalemate threat makes it impossible for White to win.

Diagram 290

Black to move.
With the Black King far away, the Bishop Pawn draws because of White's stalemate resource.

WHITE	BLACK
1	Q—KN3ch
2 K—R8!	Drawn

For if 2 ...... Q×P White is stalemated.

Survey of the Openings

Since about the beginning of the 16th century, chess theory has been the subject of intensive investigation. The bulk of this study has been devoted to the chess openings.

It is easy to see why this is so. A chess opening is a standardized series of moves for both sides at the beginning of the game. There are a great variety of openings and in the course of centuries their characteristics, merits and defects have become pretty familiar to students of chess theory. Despite the multiplicity of openings, their purpose is always the same: to assure one side, or the other, or both, that the best moves are being made at the beginning of the game. Since these opening moves will largely determine the trend of the coming play, it is clear that the first moves are of the greatest importance.

This survey is presented so that you can try out many openings and determine your preferences and tastes. Hence all that is attempted here is to give you a nodding acquaintance with most of the openings that are still in use today. Some of them, like the Center Game (see page 89) and the Scotch Game (see page 73) are hardly ever played and have been left out of this survey. The Ruy Lopez, on the other hand, has enjoyed great popularity for a long time.

All the openings have *variations*—alternative possibilities which take on a sharply defined character differentiating them from other variations of the same opening. To give all these variations would only confuse you. Hence one outstanding variation has generally been selected to give the "feel" of that line of play.

Basic opening moves which give the opening its name appear in *italics* in the text; the moves of the variation are given in regular type.

DANISH GAMBIT

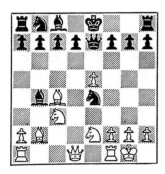

Diagram 291

(Position after 9 O—O.)
White has a formidable attack.
He doesn't mind being several
Pawns down!

Here White offers the sacrifice of two Pawns in order to get a big lead in development.

	WHITE	BLACK
1	P—K4	P—K4
2	P—Q4	P×P
3	P—QB3	P×P
4	B—QB4	P×P
5	B×P	N—KB3
6	P—K5	B—N5ch
7	N—B3	Q—K2
8	KN—K2	N—K5
9	O—O	. . . . . .

We are dealing here with openings in which both sides play 1 P—K4—probably best for the inexperienced player. We can already see even at this point that where White follows up with an early P—Q4, Black has no trouble getting an even game. P—Q4 requires more preparation.

GIUOCO PIANO

They call this the "quiet game" but there are times when it becomes wild and woolly!

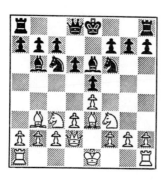

Diagram 292

(Position after 8 B—N3.) *This sedate line has little aggressive quality, but its placidity should recommend it to the beginner.*

	WHITE	BLACK
1	*P—K4*	*P—K4*
2	*N—KB3*	*N—OB3*
3	*B—B4*	*B—B4*
4	P—Q3	N—B3
5	N—B3	P—Q3
6	B—K3	B—N3
7	Q—Q2	B—K3
8	B—N3	. . . . . .

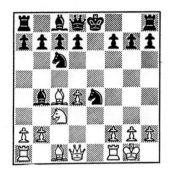

Diagram 293

(Position after 8 O—O.)
*Very wild this time! Even the
masters are in doubt about
the outcome. Ideal for skittles
play.*

	WHITE	BLACK
1	P—K4	P—K4
2	N—KB3	N—QB3
3	B—B4	B—B4
4	P—B3	N—B3
5	P—Q4	P×P
6	P×P	B—N5ch
7	N—B3	N×KP
8	O—O	. . . . . .

In these two variations of the Giuoco Piano, White either
refrains from P—Q4, contenting himself with the more modest
P—Q3—or else he prepares for P—Q4 by first playing P—QB3.
Why do we say "prepares"? Because, in the event of a Pawn
exchange in the center, White gets the "classical center"—two
Pawns standing abreast on the fourth rank. This gives White a
fine open game with good possibilities of development, and
correspondingly takes away squares from Black's pieces in the
center.

The Evans Gambit (next page) is an even more radical example of the same idea. White gives up a Pawn at an early
stage in order to gain time to establish the "classical center."

EVANS GAMBIT*

An offshoot of the Giuoco Piano, this opening has produced some of the most brilliant games on record.

Diagram 294

(Position after 9 N—B3.)
White's splendid development gives him good attacking chances.

	WHITE	BLACK
1	P—K4	P—K4
2	N—KB3	N—QB3
3	B—B4	B—B4
4	P—QN4	B×P
5	P—B3	B—R4
6	P—Q4	P×P
7	O—O	P—Q3
8	P×P	B—N3
9	N—B3	. . . . . .

---

*Openings which feature speculative sacrifices of material are known as gambits.

TWO KNIGHTS' DEFENSE

If you want to avoid the Giuoco Piano or Evans Gambit, try the Two Knights' Defense:

Diagram 295

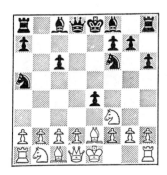

(Position after 9 ......
P—K5.)
Black has a good initiative in return for the sacrificed Pawn.

	WHITE	BLACK
1	P—K4	P—K4
2	N—KB3	N—QB3
3	B—B4	N—B3
4	N—N5	P—Q4
5	P×P	N—QR4*
6	B—N5ch	P—B3
7	P×P	P×P
8	B—K2	P—KR3
9	N—KB3	P—K5

---

*5......N×P; 6 N×BP?!, K×N; 7 Q—B3ch, K—K3 is the famous "Fried Liver" Attack. It is unsound but very troublesome to play against.

By adopting the Max Lange Attack, White indicates at once that he seeks a vigorous attacking game. The Four Knights', on the other hand, is a slow-moving opening in which White refrains from an immediate P—Q4. The usual consequence is a heavy maneuvering game which requires a considerable store of patience.

MAX LANGE ATTACK

Tricky and full of traps, this opening has puzzled the experts for decades!

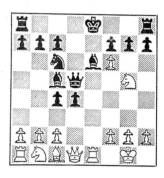

Diagram 296

(Position after 9 ...... Q—Q4.)
After 10 N—QB3, Q—B4; 11 QN—K4, O—O—O the position is extremely complicated.

	WHITE	BLACK
1	P—K4	P—K4
2	N—KB3	N—QB3
3	B—B4	B—B4
4	O—O	N—B3
5	P—Q4	P×P
6	P—K5	P—Q4
7	P×N	P×B
8	R—K1ch	B—K3
9	N—N5	Q—Q4

FOUR KNIGHTS' GAME

Phlegmatic and solid, this opening appeals to the conservative-minded player.

Diagram 297

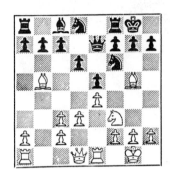

(Position after 9 . . . . . .
N—Q1.)
White has two active Bishops, but Black's position is compact and safe enough.

	WHITE	BLACK
1	*P—K4*	*P—K4*
2	*N—KB3*	*N—QB3*
3	*N—B3*	*N—B3*
4	*B—N5*	*B—N5*
5	*O—O*	*O—O*
6	*P—Q3*	*B×N*
7	*P×B*	*P—Q3*
8	*B—N5*	*Q—K2*
9	*R—K1*	*N—Q1*

RUY LOPEZ

For almost a century, the Ruy Lopez has been the favorite opening of those beginning with 1 P—K4. In most variations, it enables White to exert a pressure which is by no means easy to shake off.

Diagram 298

(Position after 12 QN—Q2.)

	WHITE	BLACK
1	P—K4	P—K4
2	N—KB3	N—QB3
3	B—N5	P—QR3
4	B—R4	N—B3
5	O—O	B—K2
6	R—K1	P—QN4
7	B—N3	P—Q3
8	P—B3	O—O
9	P—KR3	N—QR4
10	B—B2	P—B4
11	P—Q4	Q—B2
12	QN—Q2	. . . . . .

The first variation (see Diagram 298) leads to complex maneuvering. The second variation (Diagram 299) leads to a more open game, with a lively battle in prospect.

Diagram 299

(Position after 12 Q×N.)

	WHITE	BLACK
1	*P—K4*	*P—K4*
2	*N—KB3*	*N—QB3*
3	*B—N5*	P—QR3
4	B—R4	N—B3
5	O—O	N×P
6	P—Q4	P—QN4
7	B—N3	P—Q4
8	P×P	B—K3
9	P—B3	B—K2
10	B—K3	O—O
11	QN—Q2	N×N
12	Q×N	. . . . . .

In the first variation (Diagram 298), the position will be congested for a long time and perhaps even for the duration of the game, leading to a type of play which requires considerable patience on the part of both players. The second variation (Diagram 299) is certainly more enterprising, but it has the drawback for Black that he is frequently subjected to a powerful attack after castling.

PHILIDOR DEFENSE

Congested positions are usually the curse of this defense, as far as Black is concerned.

Diagram 300

(Position after 9 . . . . . .
P—KR3.)
*Black will have great
difficulty in completing his
development properly.*

	WHITE	BLACK
1	*P—K4*	*P—K4*
2	*N—KB3*	*P—Q3*
3	P—Q4	N—KB3
4	N—B3	QN—Q2
5	B—QB4	B—K2
6	O—O	O—O
7	Q—K2	P—B3
8	P—QR4	Q—B2
9	B—N3	P—KR3

VIENNA GAME

Preparing for the advance of his King Bishop Pawn is the keynote of White's play in this opening.

Diagram 301

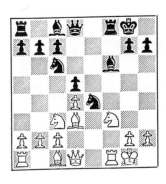

(Position after 9 . . . . . .
N—B3.)
Black has a nice development and may expect to hold his own.

	WHITE	BLACK
1	*P—K4*	*P—K4*
2	*N—QB3*	N—KB3
3	P—B4	P—Q4
4	BP×P	N×P
5	N—B3	B—K2
6	P—Q4	O—O
7	B—Q3	P—KB4
8	P×P e.p.	B×P
9	O—O	N—B3

KING'S GAMBIT

Complications generally come thick and fast in this the most volatile of all the chess openings. A sample is the Muzio Gambit:

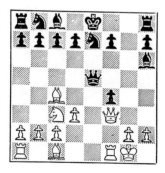

Diagram 302

(Position after 9 ......
N—K2.)
White has enough attack to compensate for the missing piece.

	WHITE	BLACK
1	P—K4	P—K4
2	P—KB4	P×P
3	N—KB3	P—KN4
4	B—B4	P—N5
5	O—O	P×N
6	Q×P	Q—B3
7	P—K5	Q×P
8	P—Q3	B—R3
9	N—B3	N—K2

KING'S GAMBIT DECLINED

Discretion is the better part of valor: Black evades the complications of the gambit accepted.

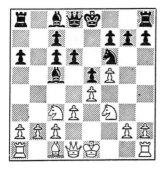

Diagram 303

(Position after 9 . . . . . .
B—B1.)
White will advance his King-side Pawns; Black will aim for . . . . . . P—Q4.

	WHITE	BLACK
1	*P—K4*	*P—K4*
2	*P—KB4*	*B—B4*
3	N—KB3★	P—Q3
4	N—B3	N—KB3
5	B—B4	N—B3
6	P—Q3	B—K3
7	B—N5	P—QR3
8	B×Nch	P×B
9	P—B5	B—B1

★ If 3 P×P??, Q—R5ch is murderous.

FALKBEER COUNTER GAMBIT

This is another—livelier—way to decline the King's Gambit. Enterprising players favor the Falkbeer.

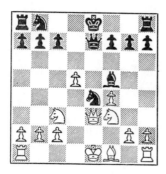

Diagram 304

(Position after 10 Q×B.)

	WHITE	BLACK
1	P—K4	P—K4
2	P—KB4	P—Q4
3	KP×P	P—K5
4	P—Q3	N—KB3
5	P×P	N×KP
6	N—KB3	B—QB4
7	Q—K2	B—B4
8	N—B3	Q—K2
9	B—K3	B×B
10	Q×B	. . . . . .

The ending after 10 . . . . . . N×N is even.

SICILIAN DEFENSE

By adopting this complex but fascinating defense, Black avoids many of the standard lines resulting from 1 P—K4, P—K4.

Diagram 305

(Position after 9 . . . . . .
B—K3.)
White has a strong hold on each of the important center squares.

	WHITE	BLACK
1	*P—K4*	P—QB4
2	N—KB3	N—QB3
3	P—Q4	P×P
4	N×P	N—B3
5	N—QB3	P—Q3
6	B—K2	P—KN3
7	O—O	B—N2
8	N—N3	O—O
9	P—B4	B—K3

FRENCH DEFENSE

More conservative than the Sicilian, the French is well-suited to the style of tenacious defensive players.

Diagram 306

(Position after 10 ......
P—QB4.)
A tense game of attack and counterattack will follow.

	WHITE	BLACK
1	*P—K4*	*P—K3*
2	P—Q4	P—Q4
3	N—QB3	N—KB3
4	B—KN5	B—N5
5	P—K5	P—KR3
6	B—Q2	B×N
7	P×B	N—K5
8	Q—N4	P—KN3
9	B—Q3	N×B
10	K×N	P—QB4

CARO-KANN DEFENSE

One of the most phlegmatic lines at Black's disposal. It leads very frequently to a draw.

Diagram 307

(Position after 10 . . . . . .
KN—B3.)
*White has only a slight
initiative.*

	WHITE	BLACK
1	*P—K4*	*P—QB3*
2	P—Q4	P—Q4
3	N—QB3	P×P
4	N×P	B—B4
5	N—N3	B—N3
6	N—B3	N—Q2
7	P—KR4	P—KR3
8	B—Q3	B×B
9	Q×B	Q—B2
10	B—Q2	KN—B3

In the three preceding diagrams, we have had examples of alternative replies to 1 P—K4. To the inexperienced player, such moves as 1 . . . . . . P—QB4 or 1 . . . . . . P—K3 or 1 . . . . . . P—QB3 may seem "evasive" or even "cowardly."

There are, however, several good reasons for sometimes varying from the tried and true 1 . . . . . . P—K4. For example, when your opponent makes a practice of playing 1 P—K4, he may be hankering to adopt a favorite line of play—one which he likes and one which makes you uncomfortable. To avoid such irksome variations, you may want to assert yourself by adopting a defense of your own choosing and liking.

ALEKHINE'S DEFENSE

This is as lively and risky as the Caro-Kann is placid and safe!

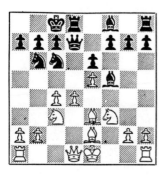

Diagram 308

(Position after 10 ......
O—O—O.)
White has somewhat the better of it.

	WHITE	BLACK
1	*P—K4*	*N—KB3*
2	P—K5	N—Q4
3	P—QB4	N—N3
4	P—Q4	P—Q3
5	P—B4	P×P
6	BP×P	N—B3
7	B—K3	B—B4
8	N—QB3	P—K3
9	N—B3	Q—Q2
10	B—K2	O—O—O

We come now to openings in which 1 P—Q4 is answered by
1 ...... P—Q4. As a rule, beginners will find it advisable not
to take up this opening too soon, as it requires some background
of experience and familiarity with chess theory. The Queen
Pawn Openings are generally thought of as involving only
positional problems. But these openings can also lead to
brilliant King-side attacks, and in fact have produced the vast
majority of brilliancy prize games in master play.

QUEEN'S GAMBIT ACCEPTED

Black's second move often allows White to get the whip
hand in the center.

Diagram 309

(Position after 9 ......
O—O.)
*Black's game is cramped,
but he has good defensive
possibilities.*

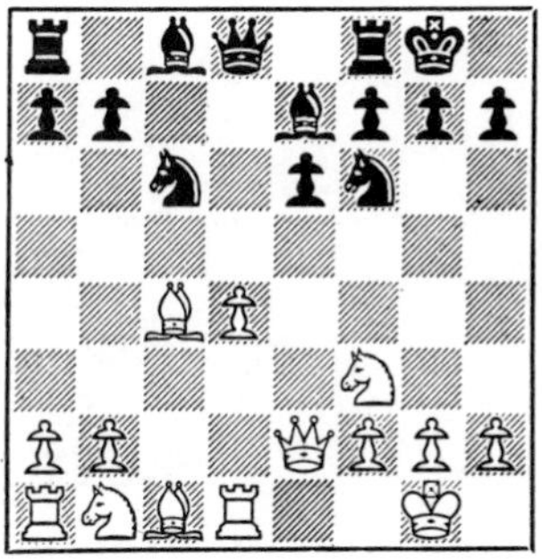

	WHITE	BLACK
1	P—Q4	P—Q4
2	P—QB4	P×P
3	N—KB3	N—KB3
4	P—K3	P—K3
5	B×P	P—B4
6	O—O	N—B3
7	Q—K2	P×P
8	R—Q1	B—K2
9	P×P	O—O

QUEEN'S GAMBIT DECLINED

The great Tarrasch said of this opening that it is "the chamber music of chess." It is full of finesse.

Diagram 310

(Position after 10 ......
Q×B.)
Black must still work hard to free himself.

	WHITE	BLACK
1	P—Q4	P—Q4
2	P—QB4	P—K3
3	N—QB3	N—KB3
4	B—N5	QN—Q2
5	P—K3	B—K2
6	N—B3	O—O
7	R—B1	P—B3
8	B—Q3	P×P
9	B×BP	N—Q4
10	B×B	Q×B

Diagram 311

(Position after 10 . . .
B—K2.)
White's position is freer; Black must be patient.

	WHITE	BLACK
1	P—Q4	P—Q4

2	P—QB4	P—K3
3	N—QB3	N—KB3
4	B—N5	QN—Q2
5	P—K3	P—B3
6	N—B3	Q—R4
7	N—Q2	P×P
8	B×N	N×B
9	N×P	Q—B2
10	B—Q3	B—K2

Diagram 312

(Position after 10   ......
QN—Q2.)
White has more freedom.
Black is on the defensive.

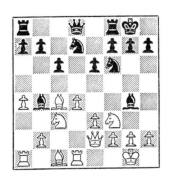

	WHITE	BLACK
1	P—Q4	P—Q4
2	P—QB4	P—QB3
3	N—KB3	N—B3
4	N—B3	P×P
5	P—QR4	B—B4
6	P—K3	P—K3
7	B×P	B—QN5
8	O—O	O—O
9	Q—K2	B—N5
10	R—Q1	QN—Q2

(See next page for another variation)

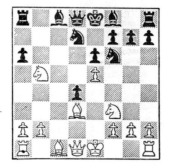

Diagram 313

(Position after 11 N×NP.)
A very complicated position!

	WHITE	BLACK
1	*P—Q4*	*P—Q4*
2	*P—QB4*	*P—QB3*
3	N—KB3	N—B3
4	N—B3	P—K3
5	P—K3	QN—Q2
6	B—Q3	P×P
7	B×BP	P—QN4
8	B—Q3	P—QR3
9	P—K4	P—B4
10	P—K5	P×P
11	N×NP	......

COLLE SYSTEM

One of the best opening lines for inexperienced players. White's line of development is easy to master.

Diagram 314

(Position after 10 Q—K2.) *White's remaining problem is to develop the QB.*

	WHITE	BLACK
1	P—Q4	P—Q4
2	N—KB3	N—KB3
3	P—K3	P—K3
4	B—Q3	P—B4
5	P—B3	N—B3
6	QN—Q2	B—Q3
7	O—O	O—O
8	P×P	B×P
9	P—K4	Q—B2
10	Q—K2	. . . . . .

This concludes our quick survey of the openings in which both sides play 1 P—Q4, P—Q4. One conclusion which deserves careful study on your part is that Black generally has trouble developing his Queen Bishop because its movements are blocked by the Black King Pawn at K3. (Note that this is not true of the variation illustrated in Diagram 312. Here Black defends with 2 . . . . . . P—QB3, postponing . . . . . . P—K3. This gives him a chance to play out the Queen Bishop and endow it with an active role.)

Aside from this point, you can appreciate from the last few diagrams how readily Black can get a terribly cramped position in this type of opening.

NIMZOINDIAN DEFENSE

This is a popular defense because it gives Black a chance to be enterprising as well as original.

Diagram 315

(Position after 9 . . . . . .
P—K4.)
White for choice because his Bishops should have ample scope later on.

	WHITE	BLACK
1	*P—Q4*	*N—KB3*
2	*P—QB4*	*P—K3*
3	*N—QB3*	*B—N5*
4	Q—B2	N—B3
5	N—B3	P—Q3
6	P—QR3	B×Nch
7	Q×B	O—O
8	P—KN3	Q—K2
9	B—N2	P—K4

QUEEN'S INDIAN DEFENSE

By adopting this defense, inexperienced players get a chance to experiment with the "fianchetto" (see Black's third and fourth moves and White's fourth and fifth moves).

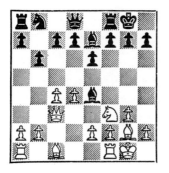

Diagram 316

(Position after 9 . . . . . .
B—K5.)
*The position is about even.
Note the great power of
Black's Bishop at K5.*

	WHITE	BLACK
1	P—Q4	N—KB3
2	P—QB4	P—K3
3	N—KB3	P—QN3
4	P—KN3	B—N2
5	B—N2	B—K2
6	O—O	O—O
7	N—B3	N—K5
8	Q—B2	N×N
9	Q×N	B—K5

BUDAPEST DEFENSE

"Counterattack" or "gambit" would be a more accurate term than "defense." The Budapest is favored by adventurous spirits.

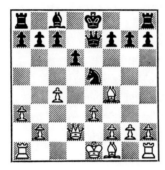

Diagram 317

(Position after 10 ......
P—Q3.)
White's Bishops should have good play later on.

	WHITE	BLACK
1	P—Q4	N—KB3
2	P—QB4	P—K4
3	P×P	N—N5
4	B—B4	N—QB3
5	N—KB3	B—N5ch
6	QN—Q2	Q—K2
7	P—QR3	N(N5)×KP
8	N×N	N×N
9	P—K3★	B×Nch
10	Q×B	P—Q3

The positions shown in Diagrams 315–317 illustrate some of the so-called "irregular" defenses against 1 P—Q4. These serve the same purpose against 1 P—Q4 as the French, Sicilian and other defenses against 1 P—K4. Black is able to assert his own will, play the lines of his choice, steer the game into the channels he prefers. However, such defenses as the Budapest should not be ventured on without some previous preparation.

★ If 9 P×B??, N—Q6 mate!

DUTCH DEFENSE

Although this is called a "defense" it is definitely aggressive in intent.

Diagram 318

(Position after 8 ...... QN—Q2.)
White's fianchettoed Bishop strikes powerfully along the long diagonal. Black has a "stonewall" formation.

	WHITE	BLACK
1	P—Q4	P—KB4
2	P—KN3	P—K3
3	B—N2	N—KB3
4	N—R3	P—Q4
5	P—QB4	P—B3
6	O—O	B—Q3
7	N—B3	O—O
8	Q—Q3	Q—K1

Thus we conclude our brief survey of the openings. A few simple rules should be helpful:

1. Play out a center Pawn for your first move.

2. Unless some special point is involved, try to develop a piece on each of your early moves.

3. If it can be helped, try to avoid moving an already developed piece instead of a new piece.

4. Consider castling a developing move. Play it fairly early, to keep your King out of trouble.

A Do-It-Yourself Quiz with Solutions

In all the games of the previous chapters you have seen how perfectly timed tactics have exacted a severe penalty for faulty play by your opponent. To see these opportunities as they arise on the chessboard, is the very essence of winning. The quiz on the following pages is in the nature of a review. It emphasizes the importance of hitting hard as soon as opportunity arises.

All the positions in this quiz are taken from actual play. In some of these positions the winning process is quite obvious; in others, it is rather subtle. In any case, some decisive action is possible.

So, study each diagram and decide how you would proceed to win forcefully and quickly. Then turn to the solutions to see whether your own solution is the right one. You'll enjoy this quiz, and above all it will help you to review many of the things you have learned.

Quiz 1. White to play and win.

Quiz 2. White to play and win.

(Solutions begin on page 281)

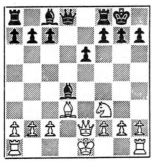

Quiz 3. White to play and win.

Quiz 4. White to play and win.

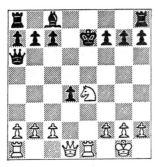

Quiz 5. White to play and win.

Quiz 6. White to play and win.

Quiz 7. White to play and win.

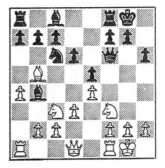

Quiz 8. White to play and win.

(Solutions begin on page 281)

Self-Quiz ■ 279

Quiz 9. White to play and win.

Quiz 10. White to play and win.

Quiz 11. White to play and win.

Quiz 12. White to play and win.

Quiz 13. White to play and win.

Quiz 14. White to play and win.

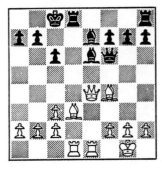

Quiz 15. White to play and win. *Quiz 16. White to play and win.*

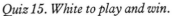

SOLUTIONS TO QUIZ

Quiz 1. White plays 1 N—B7! forking the Black Rooks. If Black replies 1 ...... Q×N then White has 2 Q×R! winning the Exchange after all, as Black's Queen Bishop Pawn is pinned. (If then 2 ...... P×Q; 3 R×Q and White holds on to his material advantage.)

Quiz 2. White wins material by a series of sly exchanges ending with a Knight fork:

1	B×B	K×B
2	B×N	K×B
3	N—Q6ch	......

Followed, of course, by 4 N×R.

Quiz 3. White wins by the double attack 1 Q—K4! threatening 2 Q×RP mate and also 2 Q×B or 2 N×B. Black must stop the mate, whereupon White picks off the Bishop.

Quiz 4. With 1 Q—N4! White threatens mate next move. Black is forced to play 1 ...... P—N3, whereupon the discovered attack 2 N—R6ch wins the Black Queen.

Quiz 5. White can give a discovered check by moving his Knight. Which Knight move is the best one? Answer: 1 N—B5 dis ch, which wins the Black Queen.

Quiz 6. As the situation stands, Black's well posted Knight prevents the decisive moves 1 R—Q5ch or 1 B—K2ch. Actually, White *can* play the amazing move 1 R—Q5ch!! Then if Black refuses the Rook, there follows 2 B—B8ch with crushing effect. So Black must capture the Rook, and we get this sequence:

1	R—Q5ch!!	N×R
2	B—K2ch	K—R4
3	R—QR7ch	R—R3
4	R×R mate	

Quiz 7. White has an amazing forced checkmate, relying on the power of a double check:

1	Q—Q8ch!!	K×Q
2	B—KN5 dbl ch	K—K1
3	R—Q8 mate	

Quiz 8. White attacks Queen and Bishop with 1 N—Q5! Black replies 1 ...... Q—Q1, whereupon White removes the guardian Knight (2 B×N). After 2 ...... P×B he plays 3 N×B with a piece to the good.

Quiz 9. If White's Queen were on some other square, he could play 1 N—B6ch winning Black's Queen. So White plays 1 Q×R! Then after 1 ...... P×Q he plays 2 N—B6ch and 3 N×Q, winning a Rook by this clearance maneuver.

Quiz 10. White can win by an exquisite "interference" move: 1 B—Q6!! If Black plays 1 ...... Q×Q there follows 2 R—B8 mate. And if 1 ...... R×B; 2 Q—N8ch! forces checkmate.

Quiz 11. White combines a pin, a Pawn promotion, and a Knight fork in a lovely sequence:

1	Q—N5!!	Q×Q
2	P—B8/Qch	K—B2
(If 2 ...... N—Q1; 3 N—B7ch.)		
3	Q×Nch!	K×Q

4   N—B7ch   . . . . . .

Followed by 5 N × Q.

Quiz 12. Here White takes advantage of the fact that on 1
Q—B3!! Black dare not play 1 . . . . . . Q × Q??? because of 2
R × R mate. So we get:

    1   Q—B3!!   Q—B4
    2   R × Rch   Q × R
    3   Q × R and wins

Quiz 13. White can win Black's Queen with 1 N—N5ch, P × N;
2 B × Bch. However, instead White prefers to give up his own
Queen:

    1   Q—N6ch!!   B × Q
    2   N—N5ch!!   P × N
    3   P × B mate

Quiz 14. White is a piece down, but he can win the Black
Queen by a "skewer" or "X-ray" attack:

    1   N—K5ch   K—K3
    2   Q—KN8ch   . . . . . .

Followed by 3 Q × Q.

Quiz 15. White takes ruthless advantage of the exposed state
of Black's King by playing:

    1   B × BPch!!   K × B
    2   Q—N7 mate

Quiz 16. Who would believe that White has a forced checkmate
in two moves. Yet here it is:

    1   Q × Pch!!   P × Q
    2   B—QR6 mate

INDEX